Death and Lilies
A Poetry Collection About Love and Things of a Darker Nature

Jack Townson

Copyright © 2022 by Jack Townson

All rights reserved.

ISBN: 978-1-0879-1028-4

No part of this book may be reproduced in any form or by any electronic or mechanical means, including information storage and retrieval systems, without written permission from the author, except for the use of brief quotations in a book review.

Edited by Shayne Leighton

Cover Art & Design by Shayne Leighton

The Vampire Jack Townson

www.thevampirejacktownson.com

This anthology is dedicated not only to my community but to fans of gothic horror everywhere, as well as those struggling with their identity.

For those who are different, who love the macabre and the gruesome. We are a unique breed, and as such, we must revel in our love of terror.

As well, this book is dedicated to anyone who doubted me— For anyone who said I wasn't a "real writer", this book is to mock you.

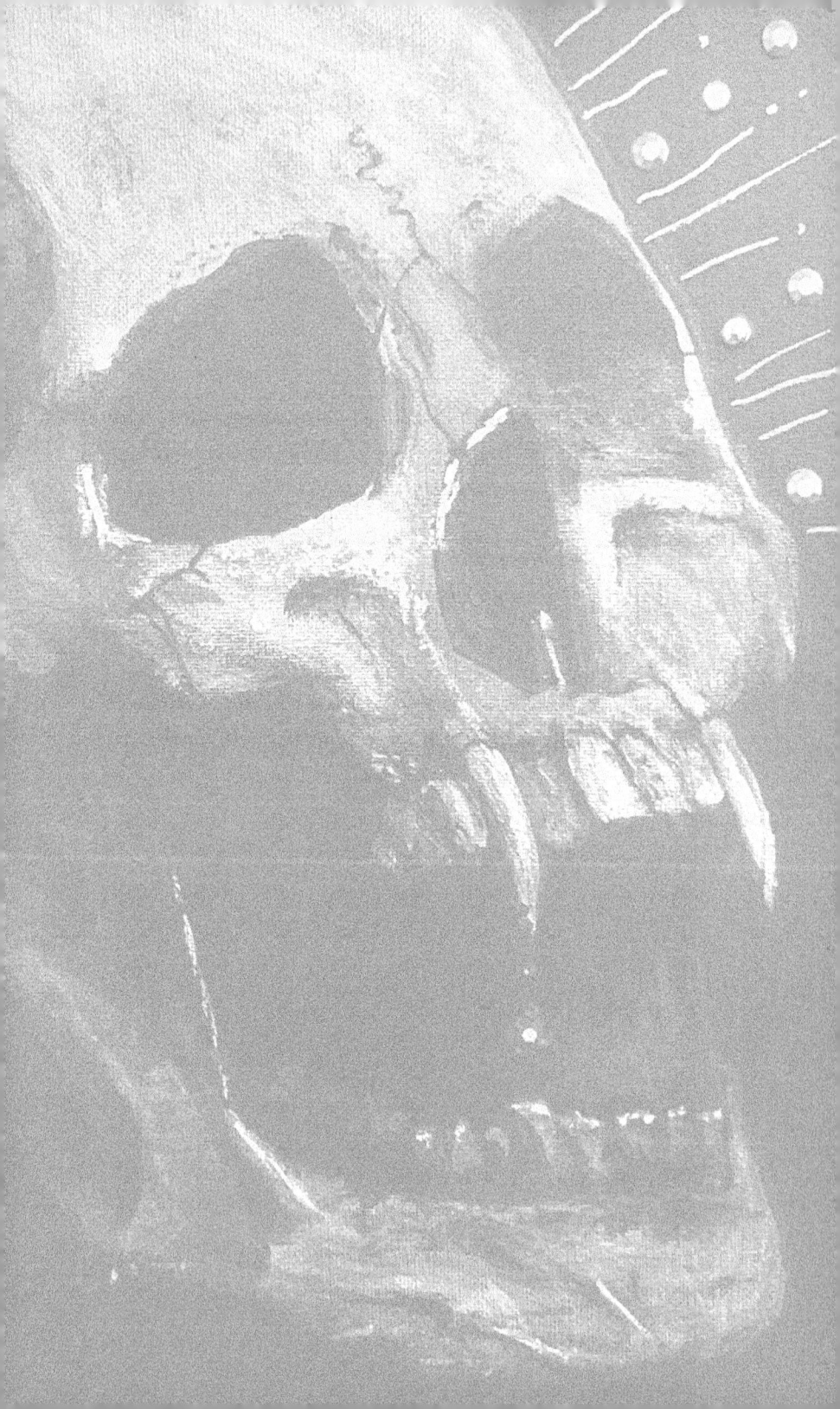

Contents

Foreword	vii
1. Dreams and Nightmares	1
2. King and Queen of Roses	5
3. The Bleeding Tree	9
4. My Muse	11
5. Abandoned	15
6. The Cry of Dawn	19
7. Mistress Moon	23
8. Twilight	27
9. Fangs	31
10. Warrior Heart	35
11. Sing of Misery	39
12. The Crimson Waltz	43
13. Mother of Evil	47
14. The Grim	51
15. A Demon of my Own	55
16. Draconic	59
17. Necromancer	67
18. Lips Stained Obsidian	71
19. Dreams//Nightmares	75
20. Monster or Man	79
21. Eternal Love	83
22. Storm Clouds	87
23. Herb	91
24. A Serpent's Dream	95
25. Vile	99
26. Perchance to Dream	103
27. The Forbidden Taste	109

28. The Whore	113
29. Blood Legion	117
30. Shadowskin	121
31. Love Lost	125
32. Humanity	129
33. The Tapping	135
34. The Diamond	139
35. The Clock	143
36. Silhouette	147
37. Sympathy for the Devil	151
About the Author	153

Foreword

When I was a young boy, I knew I was different; Not only because I navigated life as a living Vampyre, but also because of my fascination and love for the darker sides of life.

When I was a child, there were absolutely certain horror monsters (a particular doll with a sinister laugh comes to mind) that terrified me to my core. Yet, I still drank in the waves of fear with a type of enjoyment I can never truly explain.

Horror excited me deeply, like a rollercoaster ride in an amusement park, and I set out to find my fill of new spooks and thrills every day. I felt drawn to the more supernatural pieces; *Nightmare on Elm Street*, *Poltergeist*, and, of course, anything by Tim Burton or Guillermo Del Toro—works that told stories with deep human emotion centered around monsters, or their victims.

I remember when I was young I was never comfortable enough to show the darker sides of me, but no matter what

Foreword

I did, that aspect of who I was always found its way to the surface to rear its many-eyed face. Hiding never did any good, however, because my peers always caught on and spread rumors like wildfire about the boy in black who kept to himself: *"Axe murderer"*, *"serial killer"*, *"horror freak"* and so many others.

No matter how bad it became, I still remained invested in my love of the darkness and the beauty in the world of death and monsters.

Years and years later, I would become a bestselling poet, an award-winning indie horror filmmaker with a web series based on my upcoming novel and movie of the same name, *The Vampire Jack Townson*.

I think my goal began when I wrote *Blood and Roses*. Shayne and I had put together the book and released it to the world unaware of how well-received it would become. I knew that the next anthology that I wrote had to be darker.

The first book was a collection of poetry I had written over the course of a few years; a mix of personal experience and my titular character's experiences, as well. Writing my first anthology was truly therapeutic and I can never thank the Fangfam community and my fans enough for making my first release so successful.

This book, however, is to show what happens when I put my mind to work for the sole purpose of honoring fans and giving them a truly dedicated book of poetry.

Death and Lillies is not just comprised of the things I would type away into my phone in the dark of the evening in my loneliest moments, but it's a true representation of myself hard at work to show what I can produce when pounding at the keyboard with the support of the best community on social media (fight me about it, or join)!

Foreword

I hope readers enjoy the true depths of my twisted mind and what I take from the back room, carve into pieces, and slam onto the table for you all to see.

Fatally,
The Vampire Jack Townson

1. Dreams and Nightmares

Once upon a time...
Long, long ago...
There was a monster.

A thing so twisted it was forced to hide in
    shadow;
Not for its appearance, nor it's actions;
Simply because of its existence.

One day, this monster felt the soft touch of
    an angel.
It wept, for in that moment it knew that it
    would never be alone again.
The angel's eyes crinkled with the soft smile
    towards such a terrifying creature,
And it saw heaven in that moment.

Yet, the angel in time soon saw the monster
    as others did.

Jack Townson

*In fact, the angel cast its judgment harsher
   than any,
Scarring the monster for all to see,
Leaving it crippled as it barely made its way
   back to the damnable darkness.*

*Yet, there—there it plotted.
There it saw the truth.
If not even an angel could learn to love it,
   then it would embrace the lies.
It would embrace the fiction—
Become what they called it;
A monster.*

*So it did.
The creature slithered from the shadows and
   erupted into the light.
Revealing itself to the world for all to see,
And in that acceptance, was found by others
   deemed to be monstrous.*

*Together, they formed an unbreakable bond,
And in that bond, another came...
A demonic beauty—a fallen angel herself—
Laid her hand upon the monster,
And whispered;*

*"Dreams of sunlight aren't all they appear.
That is where the true monsters wait.
No.
Instead, slip into the nightmare.
Be what you are, always.
For it is in that darkness,*

*In that truth of what you are,
That I have come to love you."*

*And so, the monster learned one truth
    that day;
That heaven's light wasn't the answer to an
    end to his mystery,
Nor was it the hopes of dreams.
Instead, that demons hold more love than
    angels,
And that nightmares can cast light as well.
For in every ray of light, there is a longer
    shadow.*

2. King and Queen of Roses

Into the Sun I tread,
Mind filled with worry,
Heart full of dread.

Am I to burn on this day,
When the flowers bloom,
And lovers doth play?

Or shall she protect me?
This flamed-haired queen.
Ignite this passion,
This love never seen.

And from her coos,
And enticing touch,
Where all hope was lost,
Dreams turned to mush.

Shall the roses bloom,

Jack Townson

To stand in their stead,
Black Vines constricting,
This heart once dead?

And raise me to walk into those rays,
And feel...
The warmth...
Again.

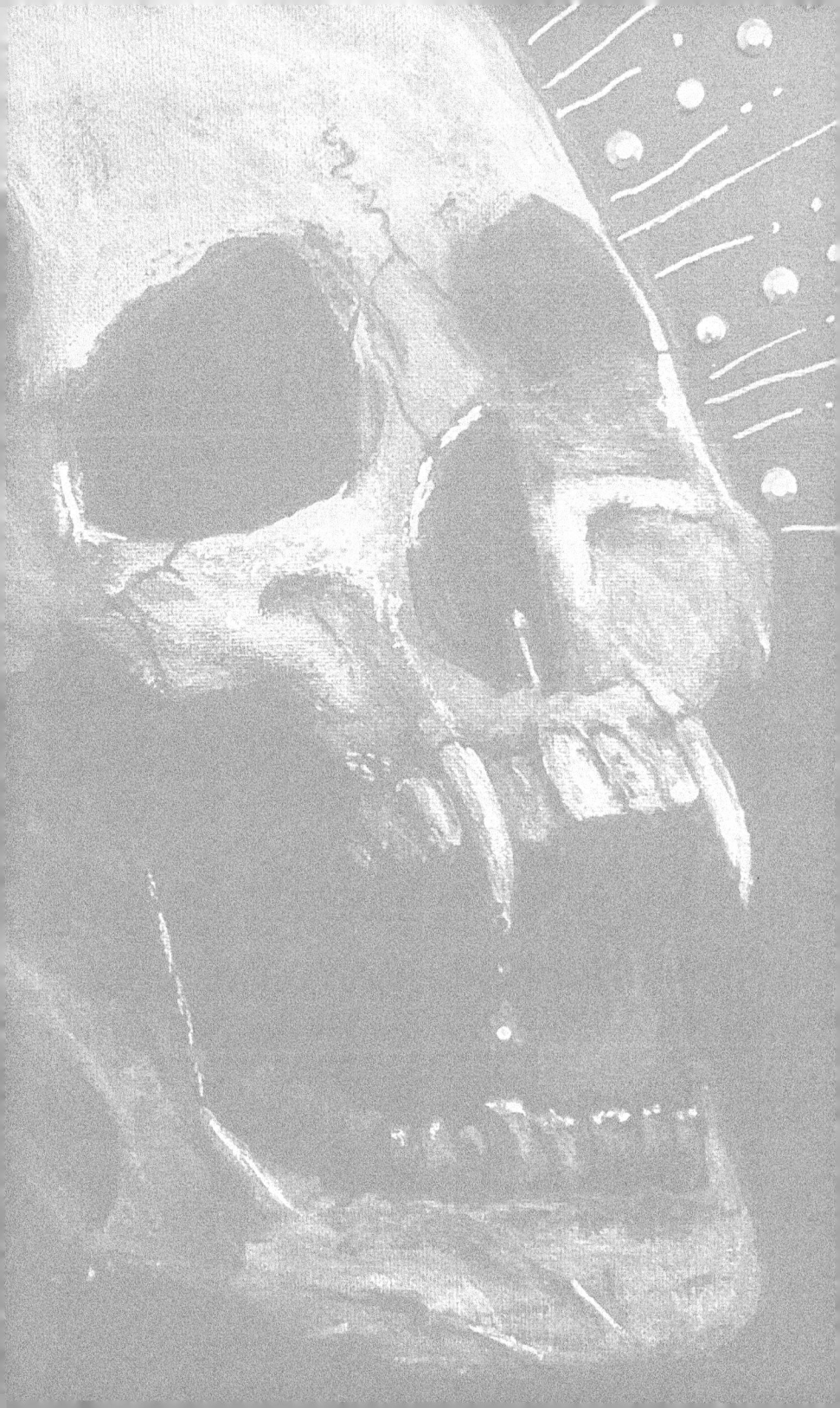

3. The Bleeding Tree

Mangled tangled vines of black—
Through the ground they scatter,
Barreling against rotten soil like slithering
    serpents,
Erupting forth to find forever purchase.
A rhythmic thumping reverberates;
Ravens perch unnerved.
They know the truth of the land—
A place to feed, to lap up sustenance left
    behind.
The carcasses buried at its upturned coun-
    tenance,
As the festering fauna claw at the aged bark.
A spring of exsanguination sprays into the
    open air;
Painting,
The forest,
In red.

4. My Muse

*She sits in wait so patiently,
Like a blushing bride at an altar;
A nun waiting for god's words to caress
 her ear.*

*Sweet symphonies of understanding and
 longing.
She waits, listens, as my words entice from
 afar.
In due time she will call me hers.*

*For now,
A quiet sigh takes her soft freckled features.
Tresses of crimson falling against her soft
 brow,
Like fire licking snow.*

*A forest blazing in winter,
Those emerald orbs scream for their mate;*

The golden shine of the sun peaking at dusk.

Soon,
And while my words draw her nearer, while
    so far,
It is hers that calls to mine, in turn,
Drags me from my fresh soiled coffin.

To drag bat-buckled shoes against graves,
Clawing through the mist,
At the thought of...
Finally...
Bringing her...
Home.

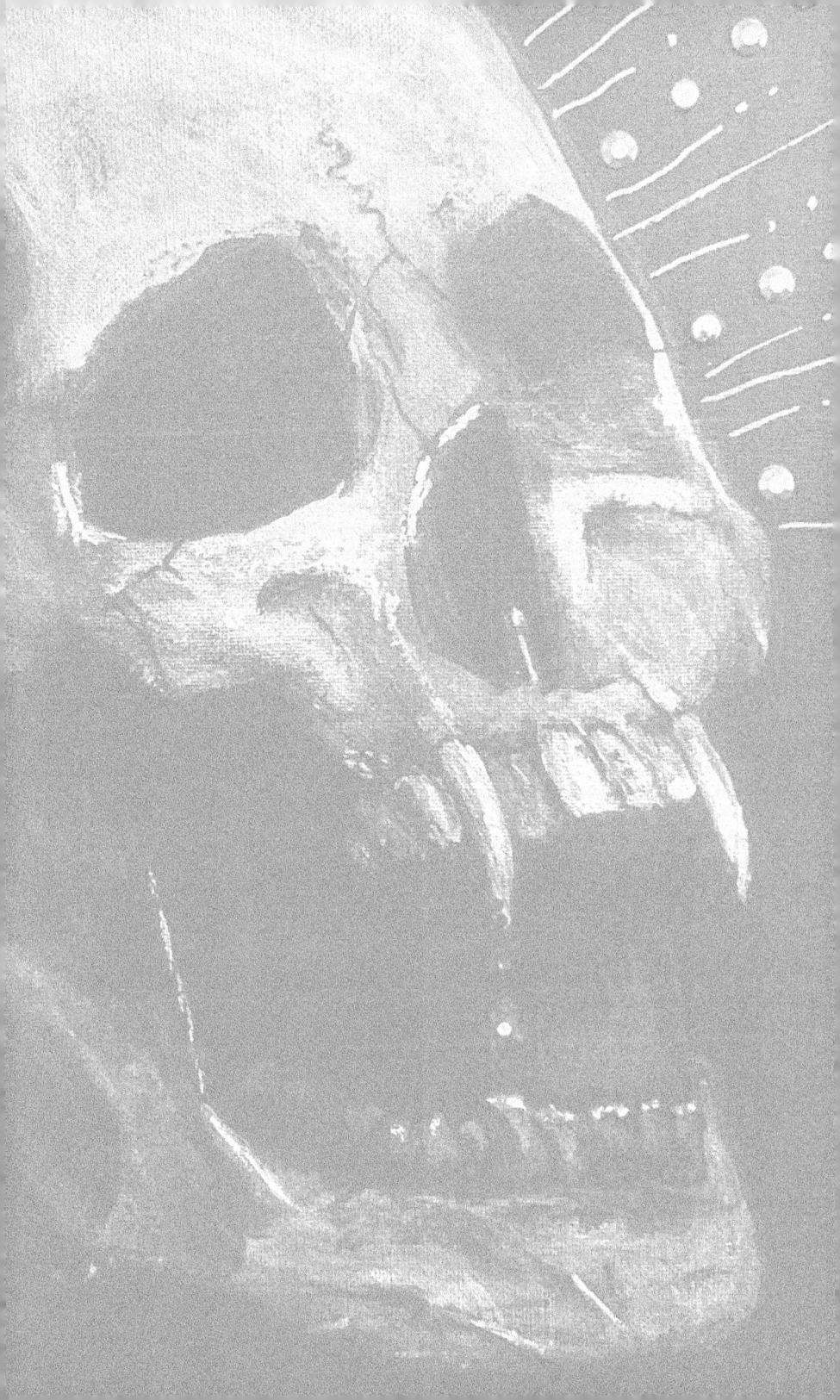

5. Abandoned

Wrapped in a cloak of deformation,
Sun blistered skin of ruination,
Eyes of scattered earth and sky,
Where light from heaven goes to die.

I am nothing to anyone—
Just a burden lost and alone,
And when I cry these tears,
I know I'll never be home.

No arms to hold me,
No lips to kiss,
No eyes to stare into,
To drown within.

And I feel my heart as it turns to ash,
When all I wanted was to take your hand—
And I loved you,
And you killed me.

Left me in the gutter of my mind,
Where nothing but tragedy resides.

There was hope,
A flickering thing.
The flame dancing across the wind.

And I grasped it tightly.
I don't know why.
Foolishness?
A dream to fly?

To take wing and soar,
Like a phoenix reborn.
Yet, every eye looks instead in scorn.

And I remember,
In this moment,
I am the perfect imperfect.

Beautiful to behold,
Yet no one wishes to keep me,
For I am worthless,
And they are divine.

I raise them on my burning pillar,
And stare with pain-filled eyes,
As they soar instead,
And I watch below,
In the darkness,
Of the hollows I call home.

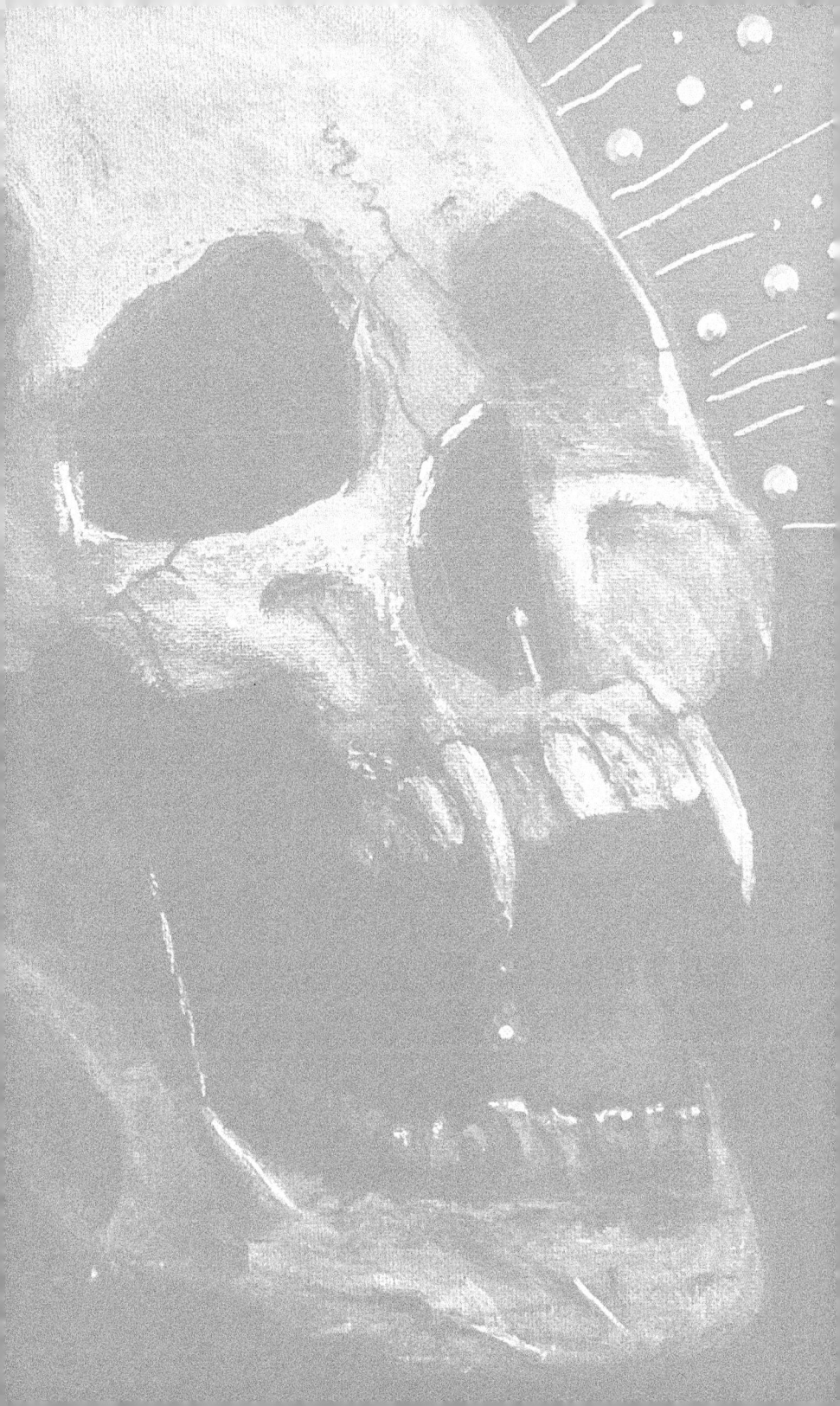

6. The Cry of Dawn

Rays of golden lucidity,
Piercing my world of night,
Splitting the sky above,
I watch.

Years of ink splashed against paper,
Yet, in this moment, that parchment meets
    the candle at my desk,
Scorching the thing, the blaze beautiful as
    words I've written dance.

Come alive.

And as I sit on this rooftop,
I think of the centuries passed;
Of gladiators and gods,
Of killers and kings,
Of lovers and loneliness,
Of every broken thing.

Was it worth it?

An eternity of shadow,
Endless undulations of the abyss.

How long did my fang-toothed smile last?
How long until it was painted with
 resentment,
Watching every living thing about me,
Wither at my touch?

Time is cruel,
And so was I.

In this moment it comes,
The realization, on high,
As the majesty of the heavens crashes into
 purgatory:
This world I've been chained to.

I don't have to be afraid anymore,
To stare into many-eyed things,
Of nightmares whose names I could not
 pronounce,
Of vandals and villains,
Of it all playing out.

It could end...
No more fear.
No more longing.
No more loneliness.
Only ashes...
Ashes.

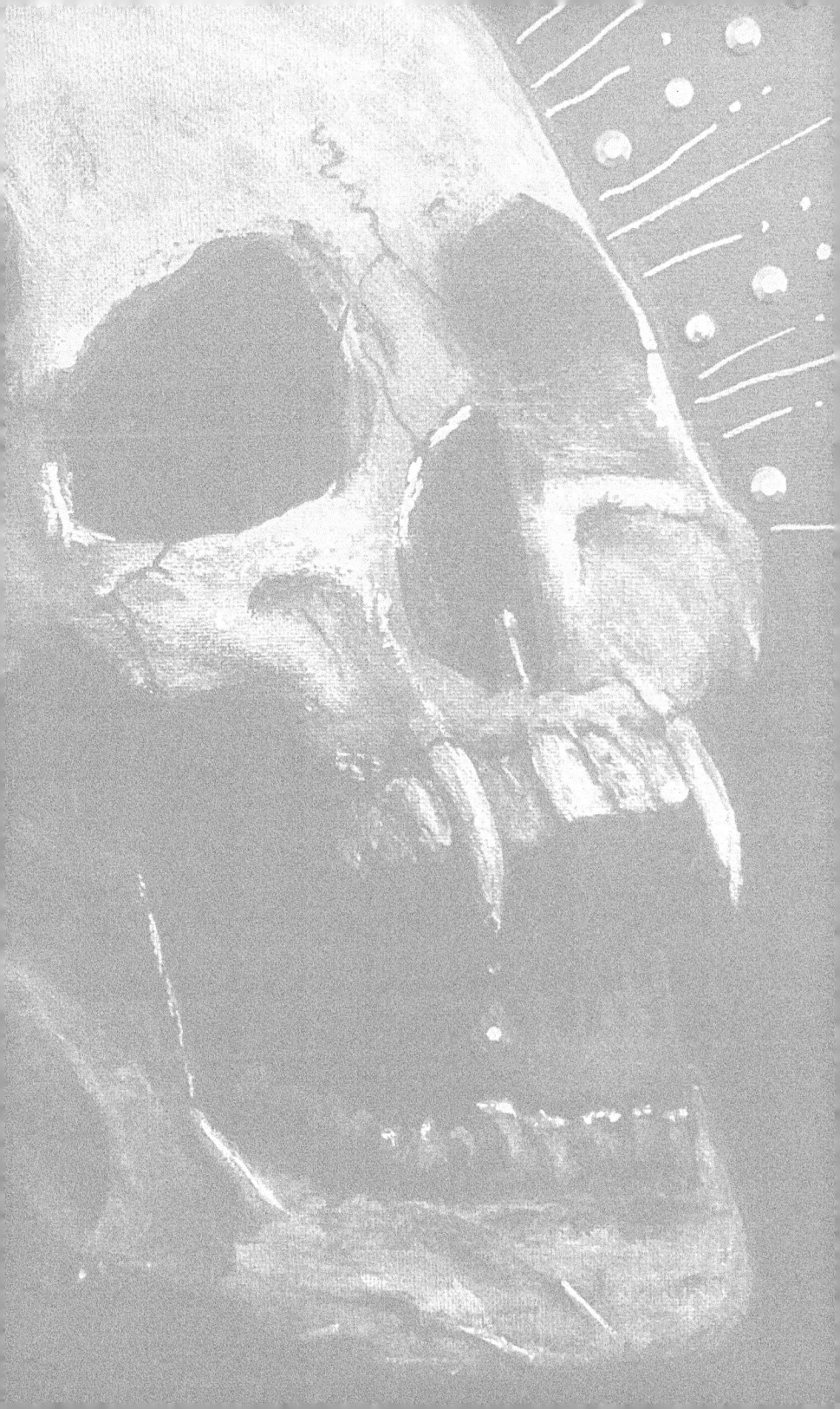

7. Mistress Moon

The moon smolders at its peak,
The beams reflection,
A burning shriek,

That fills my soul with purpose still.
The ancient blood within me thrills—
Delights as I bask in its gaze.
My lady, she knows all the ways,

To reach downward from on high,
Dropping daggers from the sky,
To which I catch between thy teeth,
Twin canines clutch an acting sheathe.

Once-delicate amber hues,
Of humanity tried and true,
Twist and turn, as if to scorn,
The idea they implanted, since I was born.

An orange like the dusk's arise,
Shredding every human lie,
That once held my beast at bay,
And now I am the only way.

How I was when cast from light,
And all those cries together unite,
To push me from the grace once-held,
And as I plummet, I remember well,

Of one truth, to fight is nigh,
That in the end, the light will lie,
And all that remains is the call she croaks,
To poke thine belly, the coals she stokes.

Of the flame once burning in my core,
To arise from the darkness evermore.
I am what I always have been—
What you made me,
Your greatest sin.

The thing that bumps beneath your bed,
As you clutch the sheets above your head,
And as my sweet moon grins through your
  window,
My talon, about your ankle, drags you
  below.

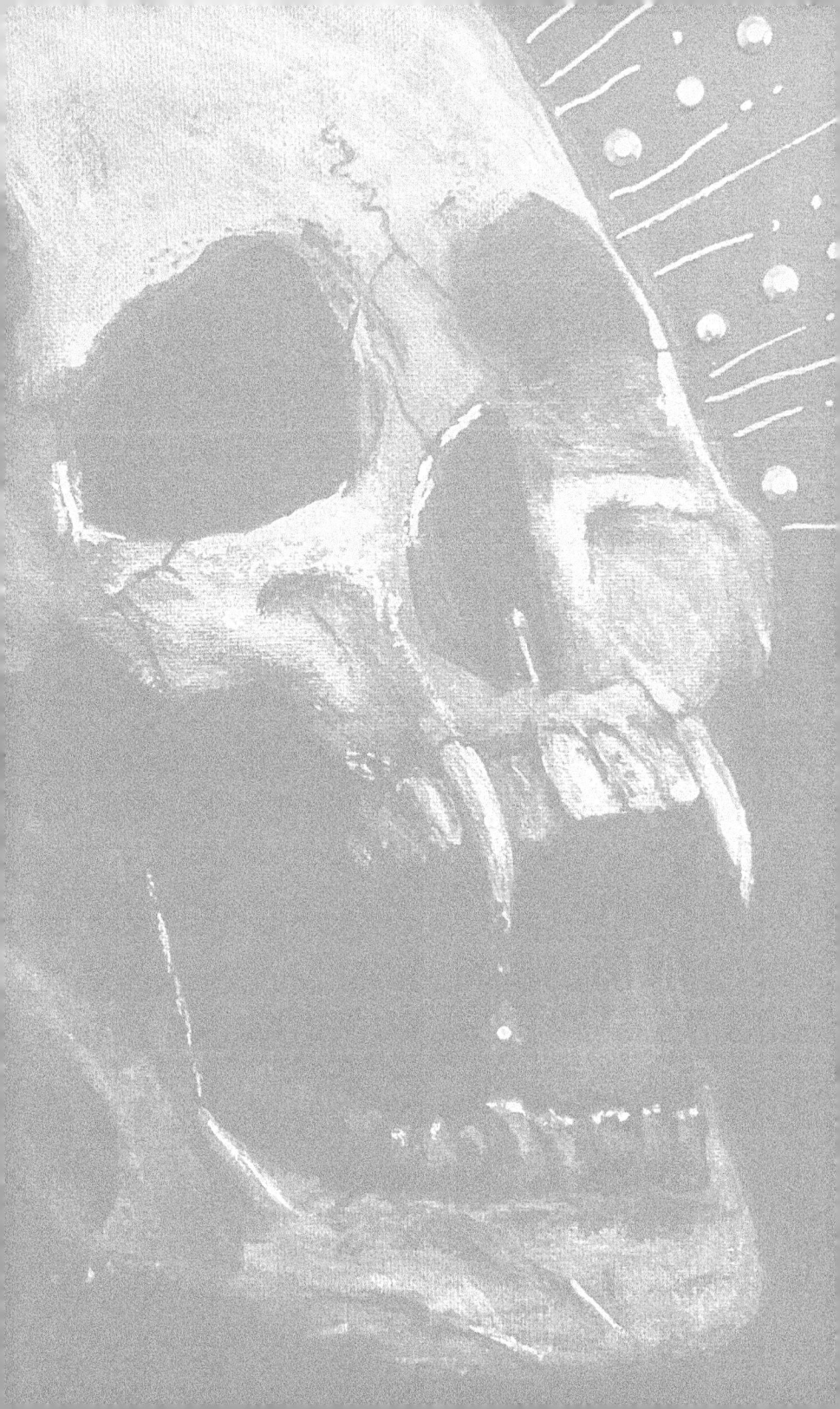

8. Twilight

You watched...
My struggle, my anguish.
You snickered through broken teeth
A smug grin of self satisfaction
As I writhed upon the floor.

Your design:
My misery.
And for what?
Was I only this to you?

Something to torment—
A flightless bird stripped of its wings,
Yet you asked me time and time,
"Why won't you fly?"

So I curled inward,
Cradled that lost boy,
Abandoned, discarded;

Cleaned his tears and dared to dream,
Of a time when he could smile once more.
And then it came,
Like the sword of Damocles.

Yet, instead of destruction,
I found salvation.
This power steeped in blood,
That flows through my veins,
A heritage of subtle form,
Like an over-consuming storm,
Of what I am.

What I became was weak.
What I have always been, strong.
So I reclaim my strength, my power—
I choose the darkness of who I am;
Who I was.

And that child I cradled,
With soft doe eyes...
He stares upwards.

Amber orbs meet the blazing red,
And we lock eyes in understanding.

He whispers,
"No more fear? No more uncertainty?"
I kiss his forehead.

I whisper,
"Hush now, my boy.
We are more than what they told us.

We are more than what they fathomed.
We are legend manifest.
We are not just our corporeal form.
Our soul.
That is the legacy.
And we will show them all."

He smiles,
Eyes slicked;
A rainstorm of emotion,
Flooding my lightless orbs.

The child was burying his face into my chest.
"Can the pain end now?"

And I smile,
A growl erupting from the foundries of my
    cursed soul.
"No more pain."
We meld together once again. Complete.
Not just the day.
Not just the night.
Twilight. Together. Balanced. In unison.
Salvation in darkness.

9. Fangs

Stare into the abyss.
Watch it shape and shift,
As it twists across the frame.
The mirror speaks, reveals your name.

Eyes of blackened obsidian,
The image betraying the beast within,
Showing you the truth be told,
Before the darkness takes true hold.

No.

No young warrior,
Hold fast and strong.
Dig deep, sing the ancient song,

That keeps humanity clutched so tight.
Do not lose yourself to night.
Remember we are dualities cause,

Jack Townson

Two halves, neither meant for pause.

Embrace both ends of what we are.
Co-exist, don't wander far.
And when you're lost to what is true,
Bare your fangs for more than you.

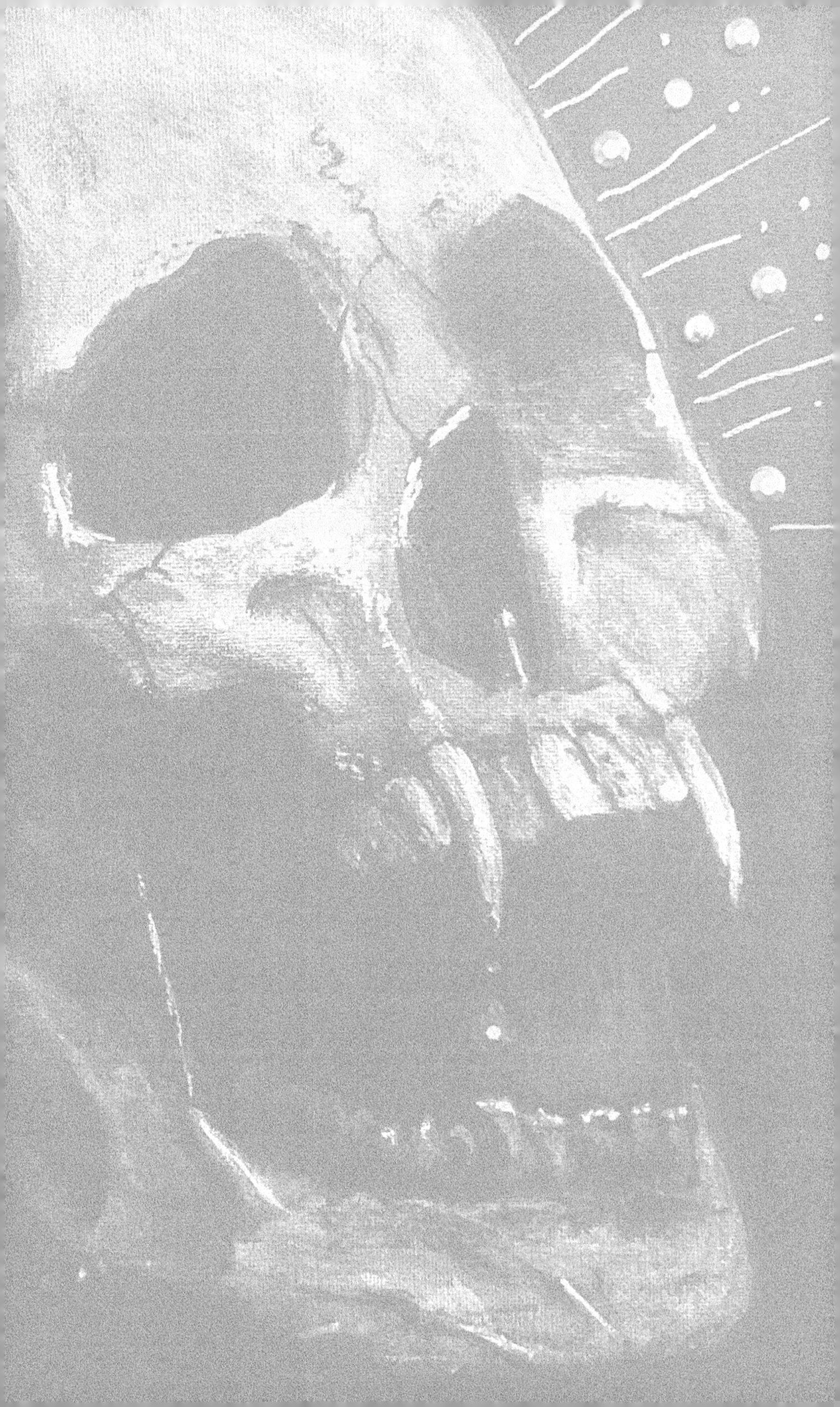

10. Warrior Heart

Standing atop the mountains of dead
    Sword gripped tight
    A world-weary head
The blade slicked in crimson spewed
From the fountain that was you
Furrowed brow to never rest
A plated gauntlet
Pressed to chest
Long raven strands
Tinged in red
War painted fingers
Caress thy head
To never kneel
To never break
To slike thy thirst
Your soul to take
Amidst the gore
The battle won
Honor thy creed

Jack Townson

Loyal to one
Myself, my truth
And those who stay true
A pride of our own
The lion in you
It speaks
It roars
And joins by my side
For together we are of like mind
And those who stand against us still?
What a mistake, they'll die on that hill
So come then
Oh, miserable foe
Watch as I stand at the end of your woe
Weep as I flourish, my blade strabbed high
And your ill intended mission is sent here to die
For when the time is nigh
I lift my spear and cry
A warrior's heart
To the cause I rise

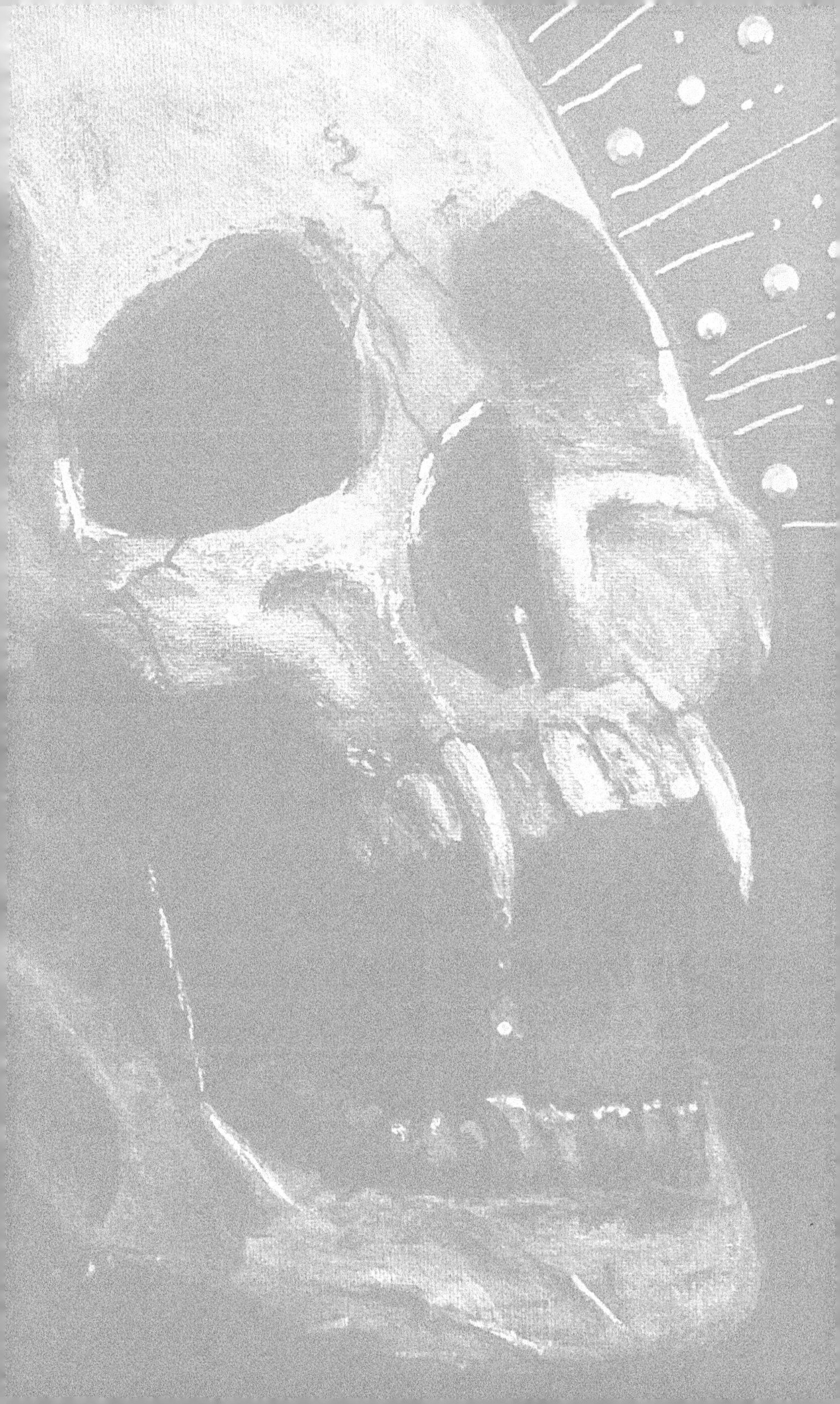

11. Sing of Misery

Come!
See what we have done.

Curl your fingers in my grasp.
Allow the pull, let fear pass.

Sing the song of ancient doom,
As we slip into thy tomb.

Tiptoe across the forest floor.
Allow the mold to be thy whore.

Let it cling and suck each step,
As we waltz to our own death.

Spin the mist about your form.
Dance, oh dance! For this, our moor—

Let the stars fall,

Collide with dirt.
As the cemetery becomes your hearth.

Sing the song!
Sing, oh sing!
Let it fill you,
This accursed thing.

This dreaded song,
Pulled to the corpses through the throng.

They are we—
We are them.

So we sing, dear love,
To rejoin them!

Scream in passion o' death!
O' loss!

For we all soon rejoin the moss,
And in our final moments, dear,
We sing a song so loud and clear,
That even the dead soon come to rise,
At the misery that we surmise.

It comes, it comes,
Dear, won't you see?
A song of woe,
And misery.

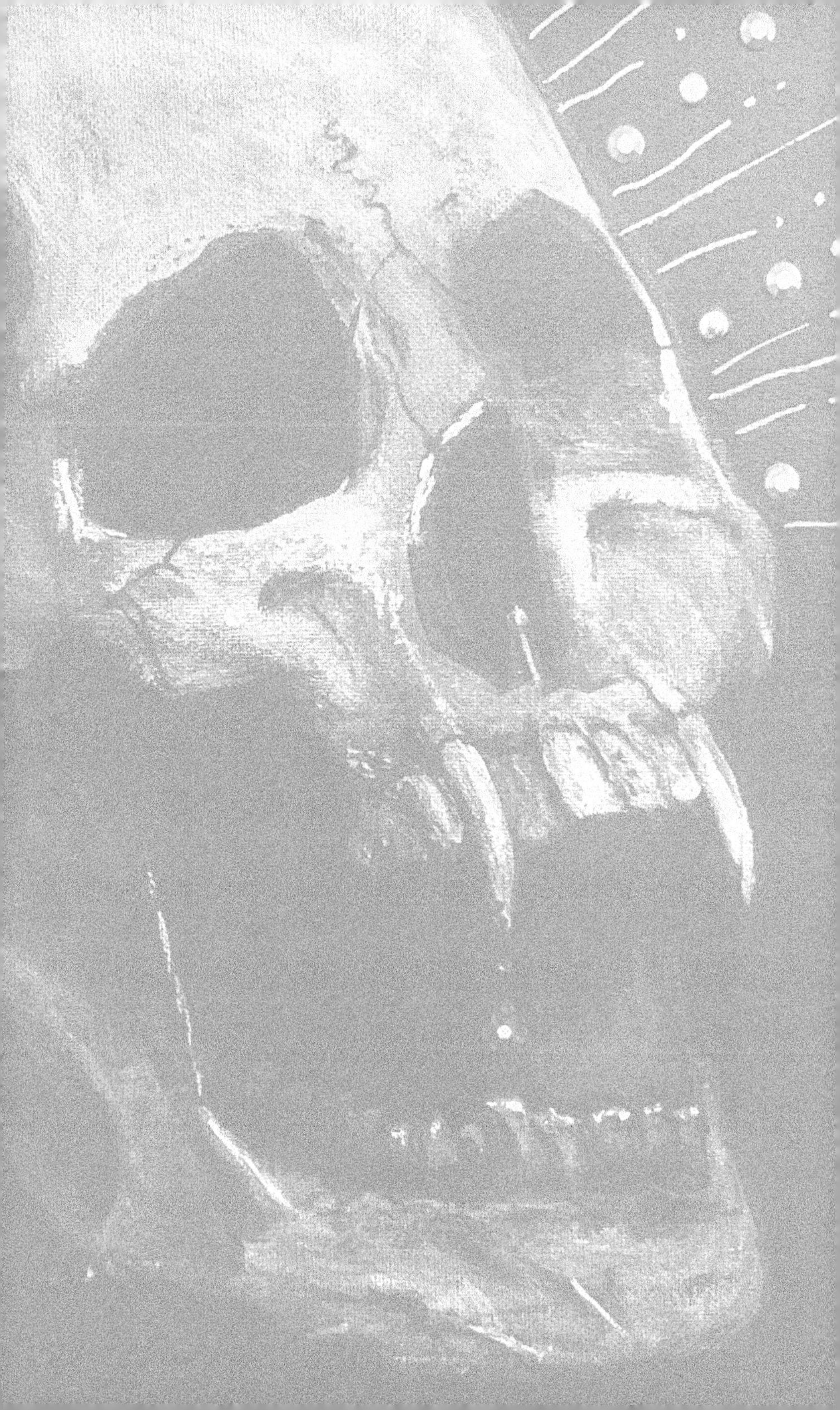

12. The Crimson Waltz

Your hand in mine,
We lunge and spin,
Casting shallow shadows,
At the candle's whim.

My orbs on yours,
I drink you down,
Your essence, my presence,
For you to drown.

To dive deep beneath,
Each sultry wave,
Of this kiss, I give,
For you I save.

Across this floor,
Each daunted step,
A flourish, to nourish,
Your bated breath.

Jack Townson

I dip you low,
To catch your stare,
Your neck, at my beck,
For you to bear.

And in this moment,
You wax and wane,
Waves of pleasure,
And sundry pains.

Lids they flutter,
Amidst each gasp,
As you melt within,
My ivory grasp.

Here in the darkness,
You are mine,
And we spin, and spin,
A dance divine.

As ruby streams,
On your soul, I dine,
We lose ourselves,
Until we die.

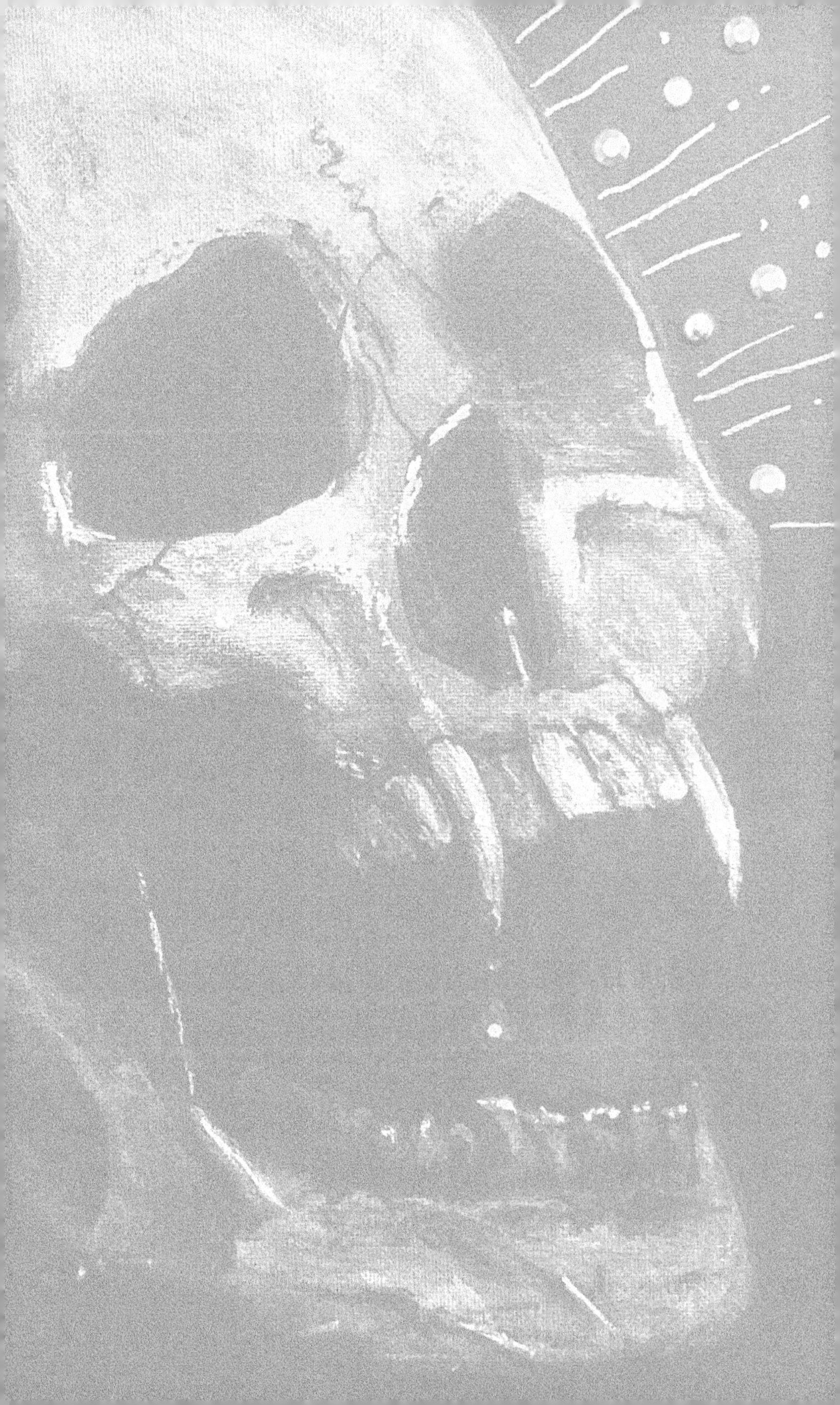

13. Mother of Evil

Thighs bound, constricted,
To crush into place,
For the dutiful dedicant,
To smother thine face.

To steal air from lungs,
Removing his chaste,
His former decree,
Strewn across the face.

Of the floor they adorn,
With impassions disgrace,
She cackles and chitters,
As she laps up each wave.

Of the seed that he spills,
"There's no need for escape."
She keeps him quiet, her pet,
To writhe on his base.

*Until she gets what she yearns,
A finalities taste,
Where he begs and he squirms,
"Just one last, with haste."*

*Each cry, a muffled whimper,
His innocence displaced,
A hand to his throat,
His loins does she baste.*

*Loose lips,
Rolling hips,
Until the explosion rips...
Purpose served.*

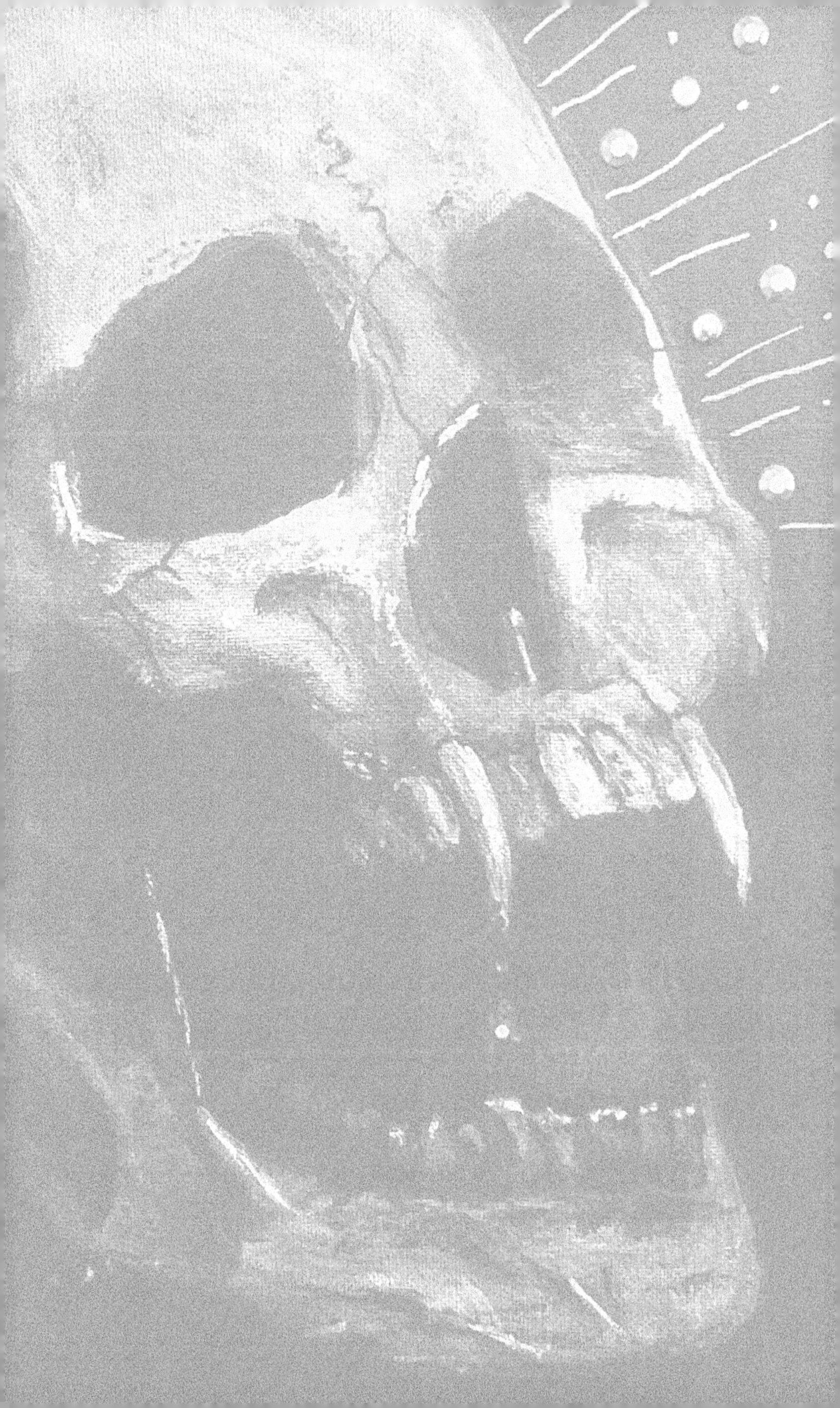

14. The Grim

"Fairytales", they said,
As you rested in bed.
All your fears fluttering to the top,
In the darkness, you heard...
Every last word,

And absorbed every last drop,
Of the stories they'd tell,
Of fiends clawed from hell,
And the fae folk who live in the rot:

Yellow-eyed things,
And many clawed beings,
Coming to take you to trot.

And you rolled in your sheets,
Grinding your teeth,
And prayed none would find your soft spot.

Jack Townson

Your sanctum—your room,
Away from the gloom,
Of the vale where all is for naught.

Said cloth is tugged,
To keep your form snugged,
As your stomach is twisted in knots.

Then from the door,
Across the wood floor,
Comes once, twice, and then a third knock.

It isn't your father,
Or your dear, doting mother,
To speak of the lessons they taught.

No, little thing,
You hear the bells ring,
As the doorknob twists past the lock.

There, in your frame,
It mutters your name,
A many-eyed beasty, you're caught.

It urges you closer,
As you lose all composure,
As its footsteps vibrate the plot.

Your cries go unnoticed,
Your parents too focused,
On their lovemaking out of earshot.

Death and Lilies

Don't cry, little lamb,
You'll see them again,
When, you too, return from the lot.

15. A Demon of my Own

It is always there, watching.
Just beyond my perception,
I can feel it, this thing;
Inhuman, as my soul is.

Does it watch out of curiosity,
Or out of entertainment?
Does it wish my downfall,
Or my rise?

Will it aid me in my endeavors,
Or wait for my demise?

It is my demon—
Mine and mine alone—
The one that follows me each night
From the safety of my home.

It floats about the walkways.

JACK TOWNSON

It skips across the stones,
Smiles at me, from shadowed steps,
And dances across my bones.

I hear it, this thing.
Feel it's call, an urgent thing,
And wish it would relent,
For in truth, dear friend, I know it well.

For I did not repent,
We are the same, he and I,
Monsters of a different kind—
Creatures from beyond the vale.

The plane of darkness, that we share,
And here, within this reality,
We greet one another in totality.

He is I,
I am he,
We are one,
Ever walking,
Ever burning,
Creatures of darkness.

Writhing in wait for what we yearn,
Entwined in mutual understanding.

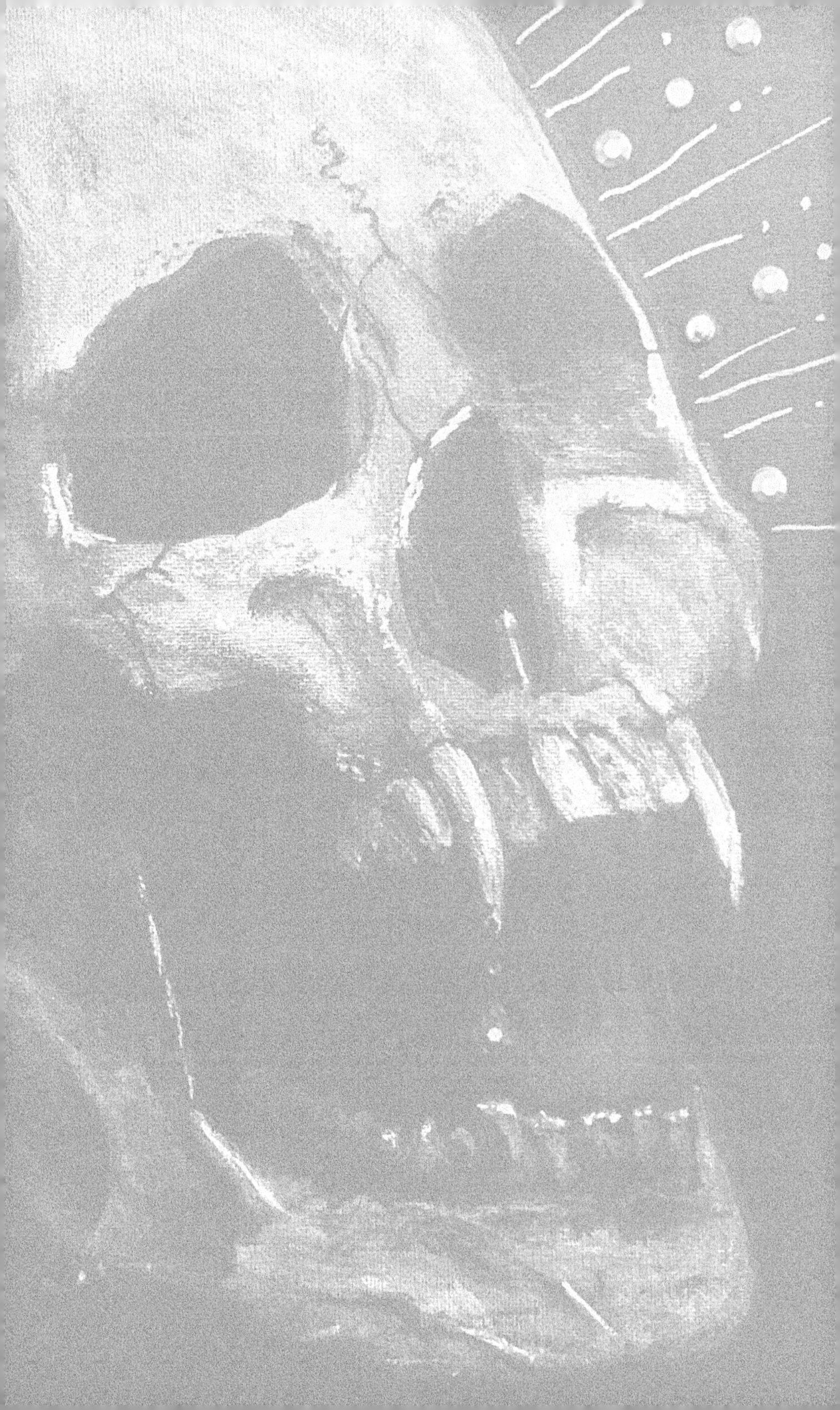

16. Draconic

I was noble once.
Yet around me, those I loved cast me aside.
An angel, misunderstood, yet able to take
    flight.
My wings outstretched to carry others,
Each one lined with glorious white.

I knew I was imperfect, yet so did they,
And at every step, they cast it my way;
Burned what I was until I could not feel,
Each trip across the sky, forcing me to kneel.

Upon the ground, in my descent,
My legs weak from the pain,
I was their champion,
Yet they met me with disdain.

I brought hope, honor, loyalty, love,

Yet in the end, it didn't matter, push come to shove.
And in this moment, this final plea,
I begged, I cried, I grabbed at thee.

And you tossed me down, to the fires beneath,
"Never enough!" spit through your teeth.
And I tumbled, fell, slammed to the earth,
Far from home, far from my hearth.

In the darkest place, where they told me I belonged,
Where I believed them right, never to be wrong,
I clutched blackened soil, raised my head low,
And there, in the darkness, a voice bellowed,

"Rise, little wing, feel your monster, let it engulf you
Allow it to fester—
To growl deep inside, where all things wait,
In the hollow bones, the ones filled with hate.

"And you cried, you screamed, to avoid this ill fate,
Yet, little wing, it was always too late.
They were right about you,
Each word ringing true,
Yet they never realized, they could avoid it too.

*"All they needed were the ingredients of
 heart;
Love, passion, tranquility, art—
To slake thy thirst and warm thy coals,
To allow you to be the one they hold,
To keep you dear, near, and proud,
To brush your tears, safe and sound.*

*"Yet no, no, little wing,
They avoided these gifts,
Saw your core, allowed you to shift.
You kept your instinct sheathed, like a well-
 honed blade,
Knowing what would transpire, upon that
 terrible day.
And how did they repay you?
Arrogance,
Cruelty,
Hatred,
Mistrust,
Abuse,
Filth,
Lies,
Disloyalty,
Left you here to die."*

*And the angel wept, he saw right through,
That the words of this creature were spoken
 true.*

*"No, little wing,"
The monster cooed.
"You misunderstand, this place is no chore,*

*Here is where you belong, to the depths that
    you bore.*

"*In the shadows of monstrosity, in dismay,
To the place down below, far from the day,
Here is where I keep you,
To fill you with hope,
To show you the way out,
Yet, without a rope.*

"*To turn those wings useful,
More than before,
To show the world, that you are no whore.
To be ridden, to be broken, to be shattered
    in two,
You are exactly what they feared, so just be
    you.*"

*And the angel saw this creature's words,
Heard each click, the maw upwards,
"And who do I have to thank for this hope?"*

"*Why, little wing, the name makes you
    choke,
Say it not, yet gaze on me still,
For I am the one, who will treat you to
    thrill.*"

*And from those shadows of the place filled
    with dread,
A monstrous wingspan, horn-covered head,
Eyes of slits of starry skies,
Razor claws, to take those lives:*

A dragon, a monster, a thing quite unclean,
Yet the gaze it gave, was hardly mean,
Seen for the glorious beast that it was,
The angel gasped and knew who to trust.

"Are you ready for the task, the one to raise
  you up?"

Little wing cried out, "For too long, enough!
Enough of the lies,
The pain held within,
Enough of my kindness,
They treat it a sin.

"Enough of my words,
They fall on deaf ears,
Enough of my pain,
I'll show them their fears.

"I'll be what they said,
Every lie, every truth,
And I'll dance in the darkness,
Down here, with you."

And the dragon laughed,
"Good boy, good.
It's time to change
Just as you should."

And as little wing sat,
He saw the truth still,
His feathers blackened,
His eyes, red as hell.

Jack Townson

Hair of golden blonde and wheat,
Twisting shadow, to snuff out the heat,
A fallen prince of the place in the dark,
His true form revealed, to stifle his heart;

No more would they shun him,
No more would he care,
He would be his own master,
And rise from his lair.

Chains no more,
Their slave would be free!
As they watch now in horror,
From what they've unleashed.

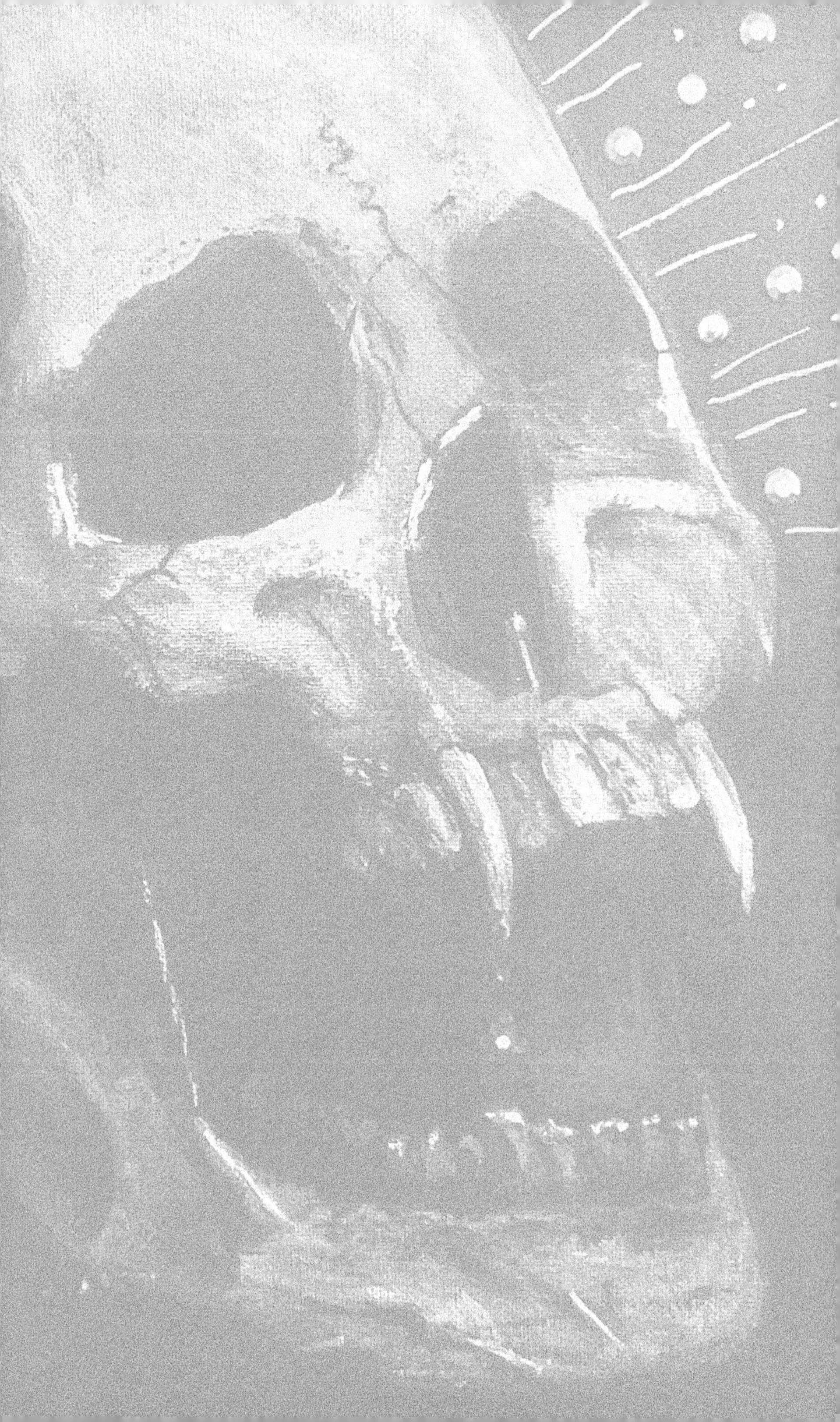

17. Necromancer

Dine on the festering innards of the wood,
Gurgle as they chew through bone and sinew,
Scream to the darkness of the old ways,
Abyssal obscenities too horrible to mention.

Clawed tips bend and snap upon descent,
To pull unearthed soil into calloused palms.
Orbs roll with the hiss of a serpent,
Whites reflecting the crescent as it barrels.

What have we done?
What have I become?

Crawling through murk and mire,
Screams of putrid desire.
The headstones breaching from the mounds,
The names upon them, never found.

A place deplorable and dark,

Perfect for what my black soul harks;

I pull—
They weep.
The souls I keep.

Let them groan unceremonious tones:
Moans of rot and exposed bone.
Teeth they clatter chatter still,
As they rise to greet me, to do my will.

It was foretold, so long before,
Of the one they worship and adore,
Shunned and discarded, my name a curse,
So here I stand, to witness birth.

Of what they wrought upon themselves,
To dance and dine, to feast in hell,
So rise, RISE, oh souls departed,
It is time to finish what they started:

Unleash
What
They
Wanted;
Bitterness,
A boney kiss,
To pierce thy lips,
Nip your fingertips,
As at your soul, they doth chip.

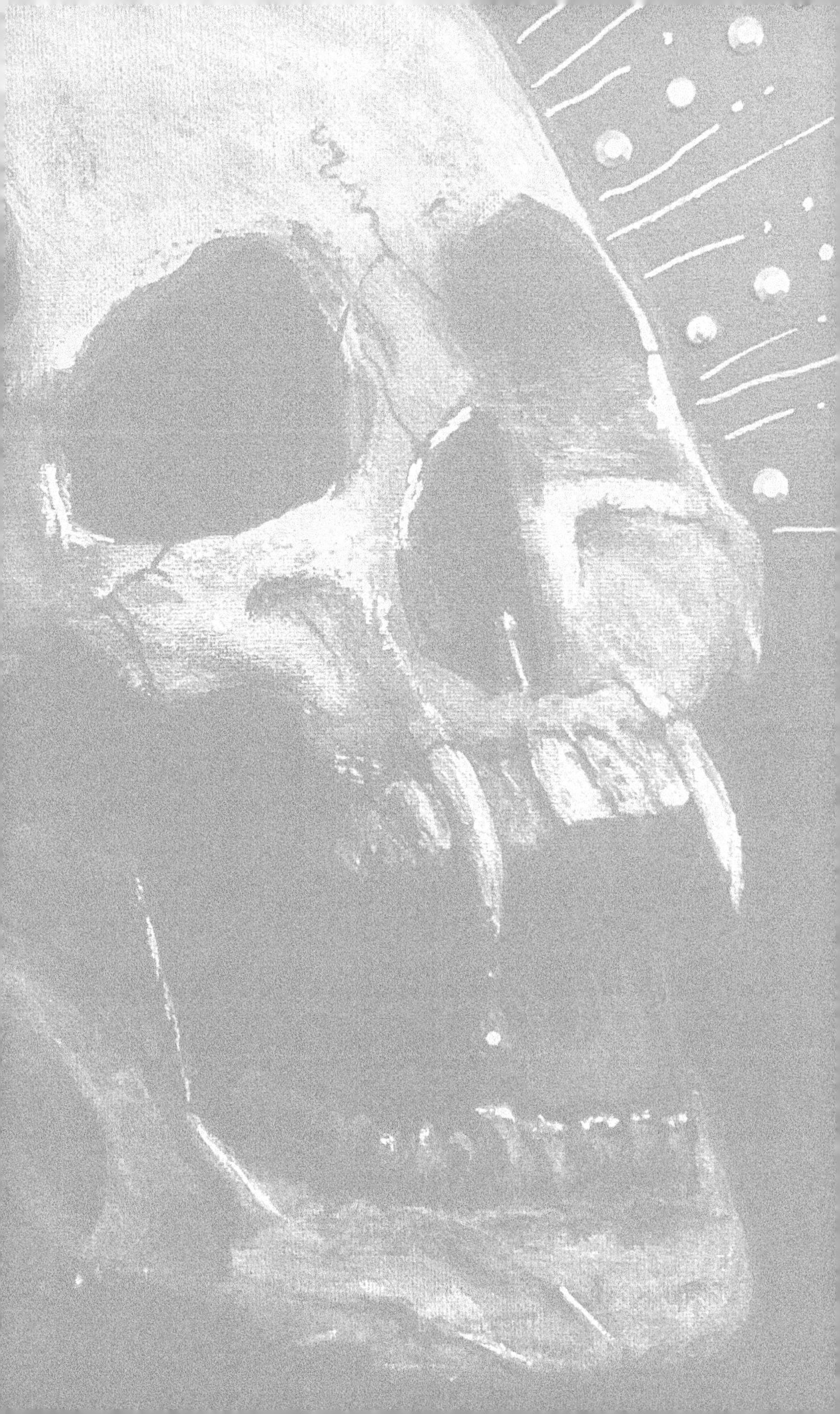

18. Lips Stained Obsidian

Her kiss is like oil.
Ink pools pressed firmly to mine.
Slow churning of our flesh pillows melding,
As they dance in delicious decadence.

She is darkness divine;
Untouched beauty of the pits.
As our bodies collide she squeals in delight,
Our sin slicking our nethers.

Writhing upon a mattress of coal,
Bones warmed like tinder from the friction,
As I release her from our binding,
A string of saliva manifests.

Tongue licked obsidian,
Marks marred in abyss upon my chin.
I am hers.
I'll toil here forever,

JACK TOWNSON

Where it's warm,
Safe,
Unclean,
And dance the devils dance inside a coffin
    built for two.

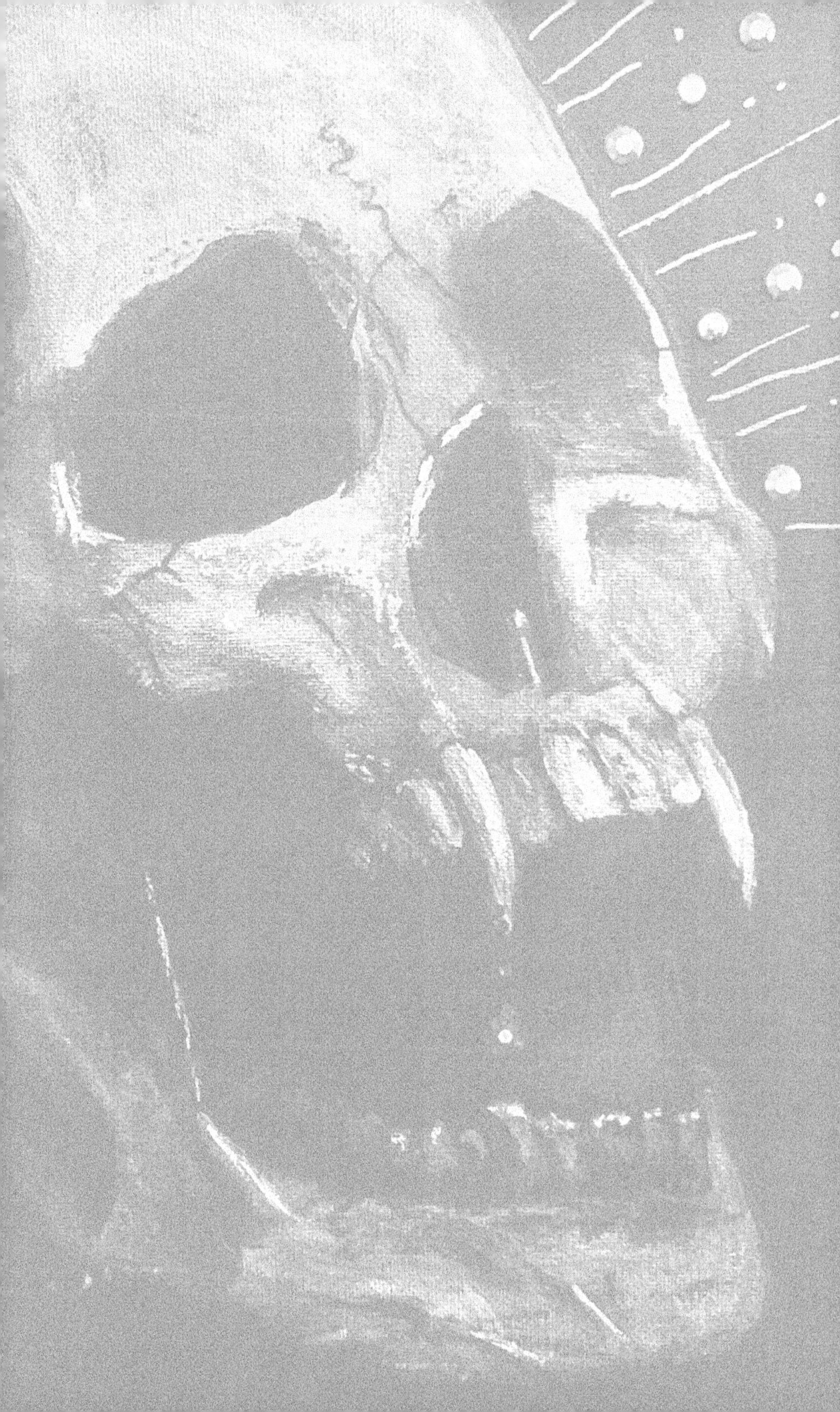

19. Dreams//Nightmares

Reality is a falsity most unpleasant;
A winding cycle that wraps about the present.

We stand beneath the stars, never of them,
Where we wish to be somehow, one with mayhem.

The swirling vortex of lights and flame,
Our souls unleashed, to never be tame.

Yet, while bound to this realm most fixed,
We can slip away, dream of it.

Slide down into the darkness of the worlds between,
Taking dive and plunge and press through the screen.

Break the chains that keep us bound tight,
And drift together endlessly, eternal night.

Where all our hopes and desires manifest,
The cares of the waking world put to rest.

To fly, to soar, on dragon's wings,
To cast aside this horrid thing.

Of a world uncaring and unjust,
Oh please see, this is the must.

To be one with dreams forever more,
To leave this world, this endless bore.

And if not to dance amongst the cosmos,
Then to toil in nightmare, with long lost souls.

To scream in fear of images most bizarre,
Where the monsters of legend are never far.

The things that scrape and gnash and tear,
Pull you down by tufts of hair.

And oh, oh to lament, to fear this place,
It is another dream, another to face.

What does it say, to put it plainly,
That dreams and nightmares plague us daily?

For the world that we live in, choose to strive,

To embrace a life filled with lies.

Should we not erupt and embrace of the dark?
Look deep within, it's in your heart.

If the taste of dreams is upon your tongue,
Then it is your freedom, for we are one.

For in dreams we escape from the mundane.
You see, my friend... we are the same.

Dive deep into your dreams,
Embrace the nightmare.

As long as it is the truest you...
I do not care.

So dream.
Dream.
Dream.
Dream.

20. Monster or Man

God on high, hear my prayers;
What is a monster, what is a man?
Where is the line to be drawn in the dirt?
To separate the two, which came first?

Was it Monster: A beast most untame,
Which shakes the bones just from the name?
A rattling roar rips from his throat,
Bring them down to their knees, to shake and
    emote.

A thing of fear that most can't describe,
Of words sang in unison, through all man's
    tribes.
This beast who stalks through fogged
    wood's eve,
To drag your children away with glee.

Or was it Man: flawed, tried, and true,

Who fights and battles with a heart gold
    and blue?
Stands on his feet when fallen to his knees,
Rises with courage, and shakes off unease.

To thrust sword on high to cry through the
    land;
A vow never to falter, yet to always land,
On both feet when failed, his mission his
    oath,
To protect those he loves, with all of his soul.

Or, take a moment, consider this truth:
Both man and monster, reside deep in you,
A constant battle for heart's domination.
One of impulse, the other stagnation,
To slash and roar, to raise shield high.
These two titans, inside you, they endlessly
    fight,
Yet wait for the story to find its true end.

And let the lesson sink deep in your head,
That both of these beings who you call
    your own,
Within your frail form, they call you their
    home.
The one and the two, the two and the one,
They both need each other, just as we need
    the sun.

And in moments most dire, we unleash
    either side,

To carry us back to our friends in their stride,
The ferocity unbridled, of the beast and it's jaws,
To man whose tenacity knows not a flaw.

These two, while so different, must be kept close,
In dualities creed, is what's more important than most.
Unleash the beast,
Be the man.
Just be.

21. Eternal Love

She is summer rain amidst the humidity,
The refreshing taste of water in a drought,
A rush of cold air after escaping a forest fire,
The spare crumpled ten-dollar bill during
    poverty.

She is more than meets the eye,
And my eyes drown in her presence,
Like drinking bottles of fine wine in France,
Just to never forget its taste or the luxury of
    the moment.

She is the last sunrise on a dying world, the
    land mourning it's fate—
But O, what a view!

The fulfillment of an old man's dying wish,
That gust of wind just as before leaving the

beach, the kite brought almost gone to waste.

All of these things don't compare to what she is,
For in her eyes there is wonder beyond.
In her lips, there is succulence untapped.

Her hair is woven with the wildest of roses, rarer than any.
A neck both sturdy yet slender, more than enough to grasp and taste if she'll let you.
Her bosom, nurturing enough to slake the thirst of any, more motherly than most.
Hips wide enough to birth the strongest of children,
Arms firm enough to knock a sailor to the floor, yet with hands soft enough to cradle the tears of an orphan.

When I say this woman is magnificence, what I mean is that there is no one like her.
She was made for a single purpose: To put all others to shame,
Not out of spite, but as to give them something to aspire to be.

She is the gold standard any should wish to be,
Modeled after Goddesses, her image scratched into paintings of old.
She is the roaring flame that calls me home.

Death and Lilies

While I reach for her, I fear for myself to be
burned in the proximity,
Yet I find this raging inferno is tame, warm,
giving instead,

So I bathe in her presence, I bask in her light,
Where all others had left me scarred.
O, if only I could stay for eternity!
If only I could remain in her glow for all of
time's cruel hand.
I would like nothing more
Than to spend eternity
Gazing
At
You.

- For Shayne, who has brought fire back to my heart and stoked the flames of passion, who has given me so much and still gives even when she has nothing left to gain. Just to give. She is my world and I am the luckiest bastard to ever walk this earth because she loves me.

22. Storm Clouds

My mind is flooded with scattered showers.
Thunderbolts race from the friction of overthinking,
Sending the heavenly bodies scattering from the fear of summer skies.

I long for the feeling of autumn, when overcast takes hold,
Orange and crimson leaves blowing from my gentle breath,
And I hold on tight, for I know soon the storm will pass.

O, if only I could be as other clouds are,
Light, fluffy, airy in ways I could never surmise.
To know the bliss of sweet ignorance,
To not be plagued by the static as gray ends collide in panic.

Imagine.

Yet, I have heard there is beauty in the storms.
Even though the lightning may touch somewhere unfortunate from time to time,
It is still something rare to a point, and provides the land with much-needed waters.
I only hope that when the storm passes, I can rest—and I can one day feel as other clouds do;
Unburdened.

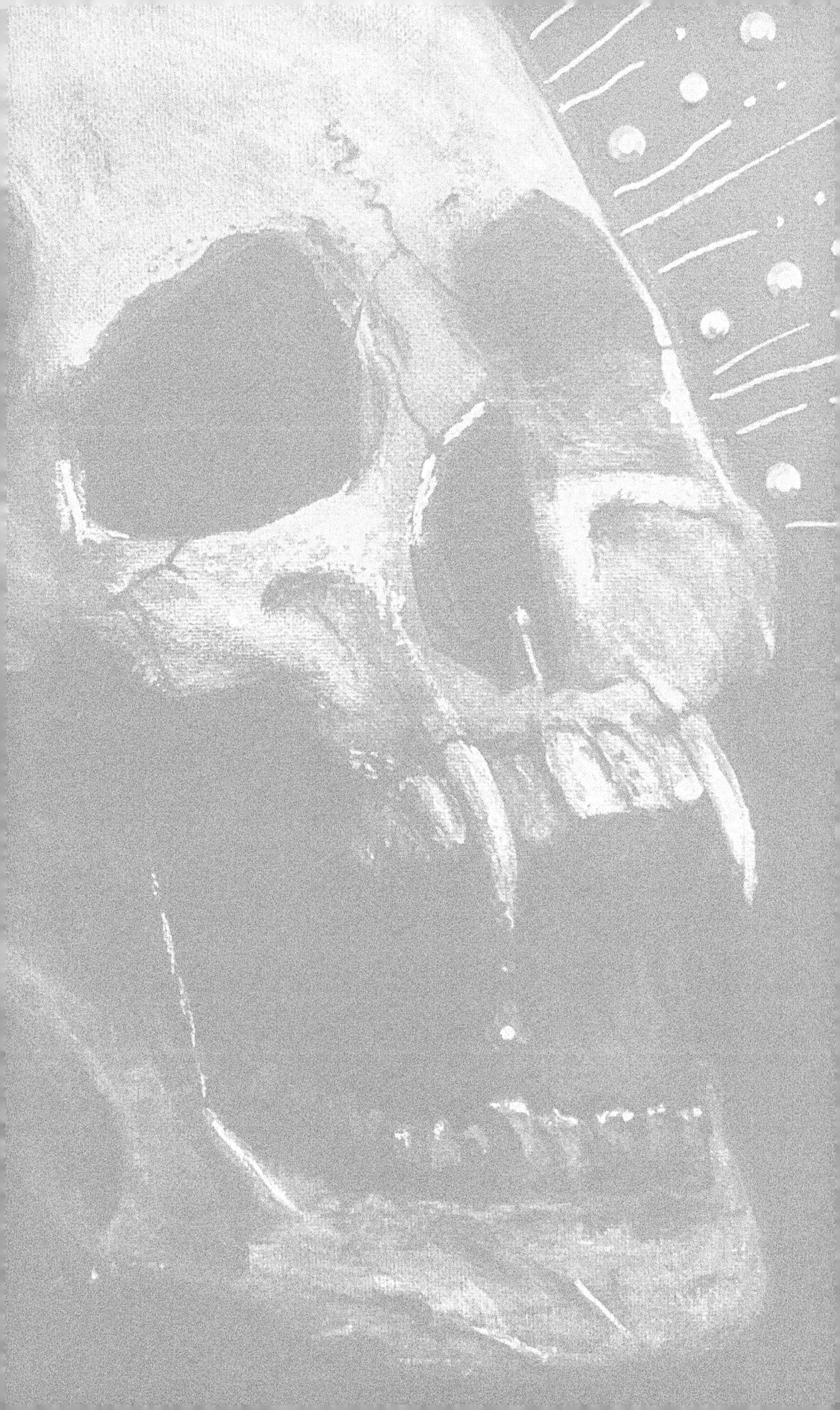

23. Herb

I sat in quiet consideration, fearful of the
    judgment of others.
My hand raised, I kept it poised despite the
    fear that engulfed me.
An older man's words sent in my direction,
    to give me a chance for a single moment.

I stood, brushed myself off, and kept my gaze
    forward,
In fear of the pokes and jeers of my peers.
I knew in a moment I could fall prey
To the ones who always lick their lips in my
    desperation.

I cleared my throat, readied my words,
My mind churning with what could be.
I felt their hyena's stares against my neck—
Knew I would be their next rotten meal.

*My flesh, the pound to sate their broken
 gnarled teeth,*
*Filling their bellies with old and worn-out
 meat.*

*I answered, they paused, then came
 applause.*
At first, I felt like, my fright passing by,
*Perhaps it would not be me who would die
 that night.*

Oh, silly boy, if only you knew,
That the applause wasn't for you.
*They laughed in your face as you stood there
 in awe.*
*Was this my purpose, their boisterous
 guffaw,*
A clown that they wished, to fill emptiness?

How?

How do I rise from this,
Learn what they know,
If no one will help me grow?

They'd rather me be a black pawn,
To be moved about the chessboard
With no way to move ahead,
Except forward at their beck?

Looking back on this, it's funny to know
*That in all of my moments of pain and
 sorrow,*

Beneath was a demon that was waiting
  its turn
To roast them alive, and dance as they burn.

I
Am
Better
Than
You
Thought.

A herb is a type of plant.
And what do plants do?
They fucking grow.

24. A Serpent's Dream

It is the blood
That harkens me home.

The sands of time,
Dunes I roam.

Clawed hands clutch against each edge,
As I slither for a place to bury my head.

Sink fang deep within fresh skin,
To slake thy thirst, ignite within.

Erupt from the flesh of humanity.
Embrace those above, my divinity.

Their child, their heir—
This purpose I bear.

To be reborn each life like stalks of wheat,

Cutting through time as new babes cut teeth.

And upon the moonlight, upon the land,
Regain who I was, the immortal plan.

Returning to teach, guide, and grow again,
Bestow the knowledge and all I know, and then...

The dark flame in my heart, I stoke the coals,
Refresh my mind for all I've known.

And when the time comes drawing near,
My purpose sheds my learned mortal fears.

And I arise powerful to behold,
I am the legend, of time retold.

Held stars in my grasp, danced through each age,
The eternal infernal, chaotic mage.

The Viper—
And my poison
Has
No
Antidote.

Beware my bite, little lamb,
For I am lethal, beyond your plans.

And if my curved eye takes you in,

Believe me, sweetheart, you'll never win.

For above all else, though vitalities thirst,
It is victory I yearn for, a champion first.

Chosen by your betters,
For what ends...
You can only
Dream.

25. Vile

Sickening little worm...
I've watched you wriggle and squirm for
  some time.
You thought yourself something more, a
  master of filth,
Able to twist and distort words and spin the
  minds of the weak.

A shame, you couldn't see your folly.

Your game was a sick one, diseased and
  maggot-born,
Riddled with parasitic discord and mucus-
  soaked regurgitations.
To spew words like a toddler with no mother
  to clean your mess,
Wishing for me to play father, yet I declined
  emphatically.

*In that rejection your tantrum came, feet
    kicking and hands slapping wet flesh;
Your rippled dermis-like vibrations through
    a water-filled balloon.
Snot-dribbled cries as you roll about the floor
    like a pig in heat.*

*Squeal then, pig.
Let us hear your every snort and mewl.*

*Was it satisfying to play your games—
To sit and stare out the window as the
    urchins left you to rot in your aban-
    donment?
Was it painful? Were you always so confused
    as to why they left you there?*

*Well then, my little hog, let me enlighten
    you.*

*Your forked tongue runs even sharper than
    mine, and I imagine it bore too deep,
Always lashed at those you claim to love, it's
    not hard to see.*

*You pushed them away,
Just as you did, me.
I felt pity for you, little swine,
Fed you fat on my flesh divine,
And you groaned and chortled, had your
    fill.
I allowed it and sat in silence still.*

Then, a peculiar decision.

*You turned against me when you knew it
would only be food to fill your stomach
and nothing else.
How sad, that I found myself a buffet for
your ego.*

*So I stripped the table dry,
Poured the good wine on the floor,
And set the house ablaze.*

*To think, you underestimated me,
Even while spreading I was worse than
I was.*

So, is your little tummy full?

*As you've gorged yourself on the drama and
secrets of the lies,
No pen for you tonight, little piggy.*

*You get to sleep in the dark and cold instead.
We've had enough of your shrieks, of your
truffle stuffing cheeks.*

Be with the rodents, where you belong.

26. Perchance to Dream

I felt you there,
Staring in the cold of the window,
The breeze sending your skirt scattering.

Your eyes met mine,
And in that moment, I broke.

You were this thing,
Untamed, wild with the passion of the
    elements,
A nurturing solar storm in the cold and
    dead heart of my world.
You reached those slender fingers to slip into
    my own
And I clutched...

Dear god, I clutched as hard as I could.

Your pull,

*An all-freeing force to bring me into the
    sanctuary of your embrace.*
*It was this magical thing I had yearned for,
    begged with all of me.*

Yet...
*In your shame, you saw my true face, and
    you turned from me,*
Disgusted.
*Horror gripping those lithe features as my
    form shifted before you.*

Released—
Discarded—
The sound of glass slippers on tile crunching,
As trickles of blood lick the floor beneath.

My princess—
Who I yearned for,
*Leaving me in the dark to nurse the bruises
    turning my icy skin purple.*

"A monster," she howled!
And I knew in that moment:
That I could not have what I craved most.

Not the taste of her soul,
Or her blood on my lips.
Alas, only the heart—
That throbbing organ,
Drumming in her chest furiously.

Not in its physicality,

Yet, in what it represents...

Love.
Sweet love,
Of which I had never felt,
Was never given.

I clawed for it.
She believed I would go through her ribcage
    to attain it.

No!
Never.
She was mine.
To harm such a thing,
So precious, so important...
Would be the death of me.

She fled my sight,
Gone.
Like the night as the dawn splits the sky with
    radiant fire.
Gone.
Like the world as I held it in my hands.

And so,
In her absence,
I closed my eyes, shut them tightly,
To allow a slumber to take me from the
    cruelty,
Stealing me from my waking nightmare
    and plunging me into a dream.

In that dream, I saw her face;
Freckled rose-tinted cheeks,
Eyes of an apple in the early autumn,
And hair like the phoenix born again.
In my dream, she took my hand...
And I was never alone.

She saw my face,
My true form,
Blackened eyes,
Cold pale skin,
Hooked claws,
And she simply smiled.

Like a bird as it views a small worm—
"I think I'll eat you now."
And she accepted me,
Devouring me, instead.
Our essences become one.

When I awoke,
Much to my surprise,
She was there
To steal me from my nightmares,
And return blessed fire to me in some form.

She knelt close,
And in her hand,
An offering of her heart.

And to think,
I didn't need to go through her
To attain it.

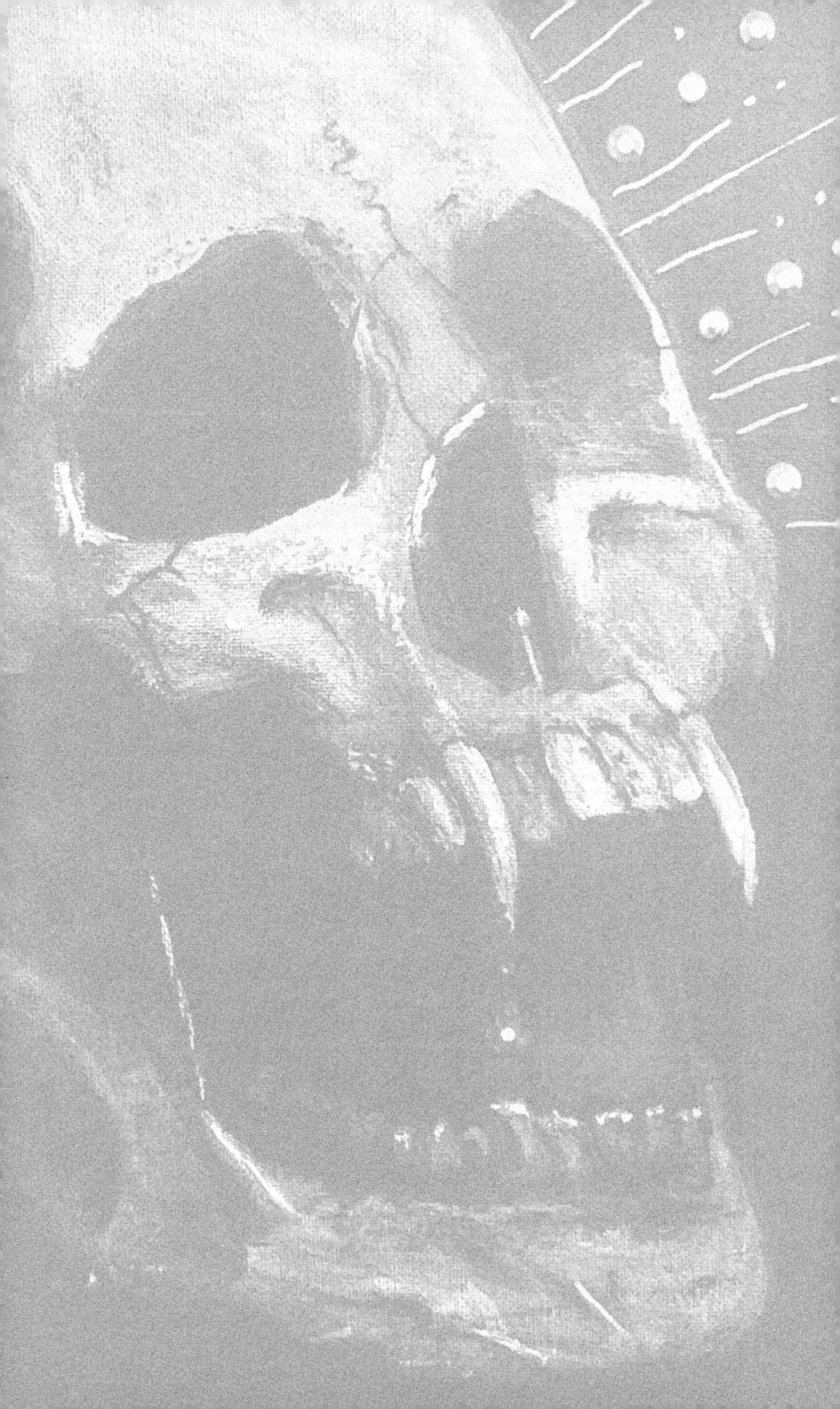

27. The Forbidden Taste

Dragging my tongue against your skin,
Your pearly whites bite hard into plump
    pillows,
Eyes escaping to the darkness of your
    cranium.

While you hide, I trace gentle bites to keep
    you guessing,
Once euphoria takes you, small mounds of
    cold pricking high...

I take my chance—
Sinking my fangs deep into that slender
    nape,
Dragging out every rushing ounce as it
    surges to meet my tongue.

I lap, like a kitten in from the alley met with
    a fresh saucer of milk.

JACK TOWNSON

> *Instead of the bleach whites, reds meet me as
>   I am no feline:*
>
> *I am a serpent with mouse in jaw,
> Pushing waves of pressure onto you as your
>   chest heaves in ecstasy.*
>
> *I laugh.
> You shudder.
> A trickle travels,
> Melding with saliva in the pit of your collar,
> And your world slips away.*

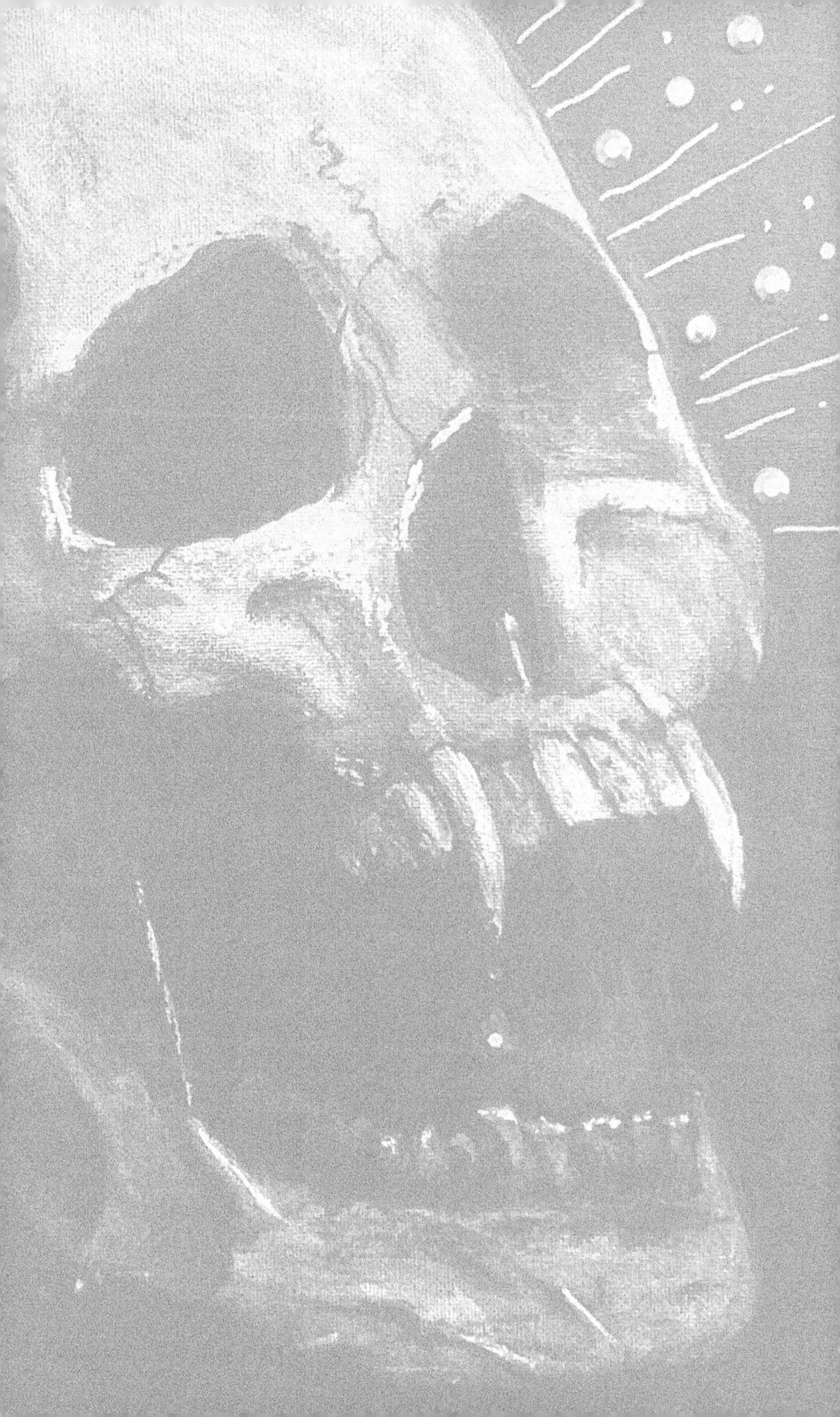

28. The Whore

I am the body writhing against the wall—
Slicked wet skin,
Eyes filled with mourn.

Your hands eradicate my skin,
Rippling pectorals, core of sin,
Tongue lashed against my steel.

You love it, but only as much as you care to.
On the surface, I deserve this.
So I take it all in.

I am a broken flower on the edge of your lawn,
Trampled by muddy shoes, yet still holding color.

Still
Broken.

And these petals;
The ones you pick and toss to the side,
They won't grow back.
Left stranded upon freshly mowed grass,
Blown into the wind and scattered out of
    existence.

I moan...
You grin.
I die.
This is all I was—
All I am.

Your shattered rose for you to play with,
To pick up—
Only...
When you want.

Left fallen until the next time you wish to
    hold me.
So I'll be what you want me to be;
This filthy flower:
Depowered
Unshowered
Unclean in the hands
Of you.

No.

I won't be.

As you cling to pull another petal I snap,
Hand wrenching your wrist,

Fangs in your neck,
You scream,
You bleed,
I smile.
Dropped to the floor,
Chest heaving,
In the mess,
Like me.

So let's be messy.
Just like you wanted, baby—
Covered in our filth.
I, soiled in mud.
You, covered in blood.
As I give you the time
Of
Your
Life.

29. Blood Legion

Rise!

My legion of dark.
Look on this world,
And drown in our art.

Clutch sword to your breast,
And stand in place proud,
For the time comes soon,
To bring them all down.

Arise, arise!

Rejoice in our victory.
Together, my children,
We shall make history.

We are legion eternal,
The demonic infernal,

Souls of the impure,
Shackled in form.

And as we slip,
We trip,
Into the darkness we found,
Where together we writhe...
Forever unbound.

Cackle in glee,
At the sounds they'll emit,
When we burn down their world,
As they drown in their shit.

We tried to save them,
Show them the way,
And now, for their hubris,
His children will pay.

So rise.

Rise!

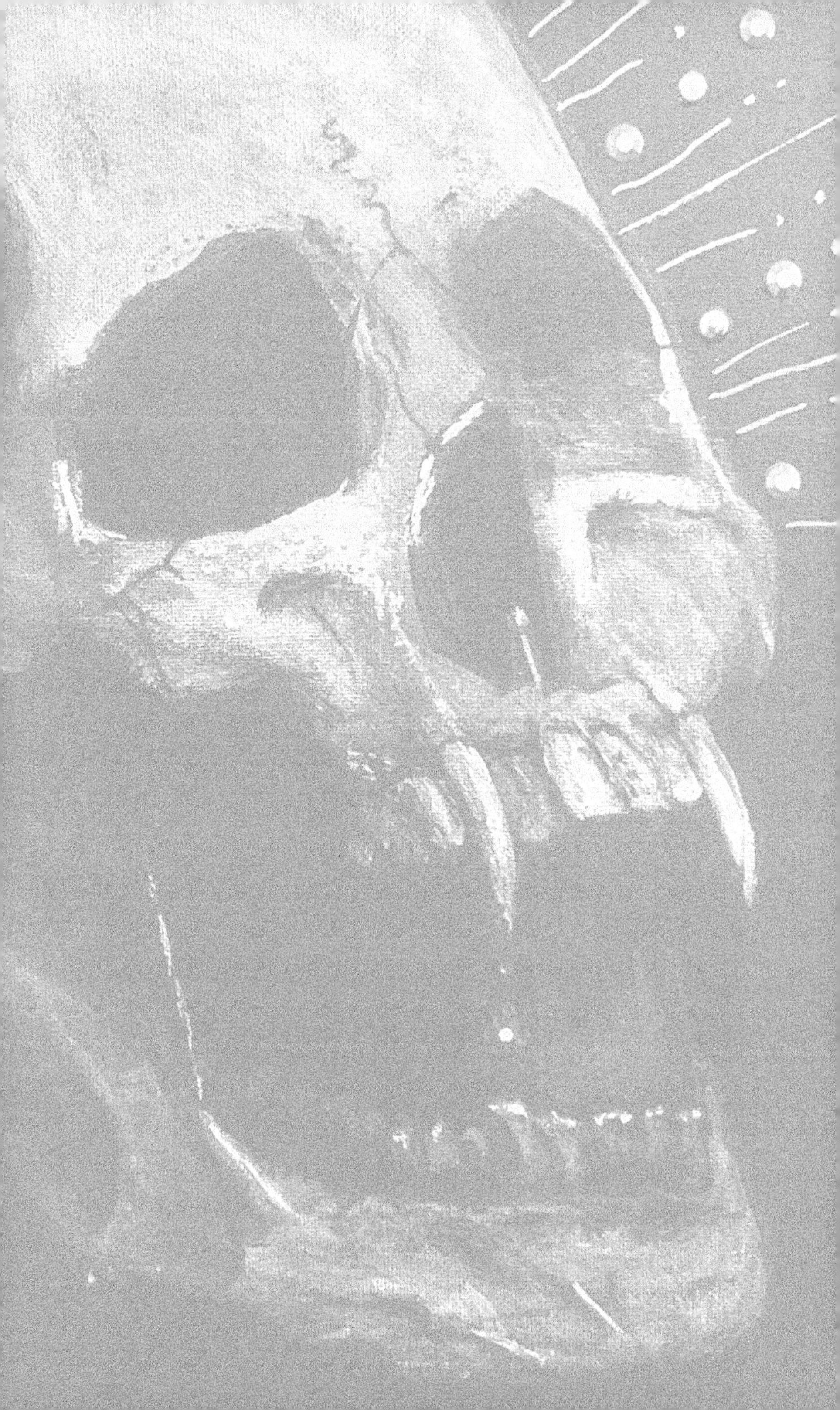

30. Shadowskin

"The darkness is beautiful because it's real. It can embrace you, and it only hurts you if you deserve it. It's the light you have to watch out for, because when there's light, there are shadows, and they hide."
 - *Hellie Townson*

Never in the dark, however,
Never in the places gone, forgotten,
Where the cold seeks shelter from the sun.

No.

In darkness,
There is always home.
No matter how lost, how alone.

It is the darkness that reaches with open arms,
To wrap you in blankets obsidian,
Like a found mother to a child in tears,
Whispering words of love, of validation.

That they never were given,
Eyes cast in anger at the light that burned so cruelly.

"Never again, never again,
I'll keep you safe
From all that you have known
It is in me, little thing
That you can escape.

"Drift.
Dream.
And I'll never betray you,
For when you shut your eyes,
It is darkness that calls you home."

So wear your darkness on your skin.
Let it tinge the peach tones in ink.
Allow it to spread and infect,
For in the shadows is where the work is done,
And in the light, we toil and suffer.

Be one with the abyss,
And know
True
Bliss.

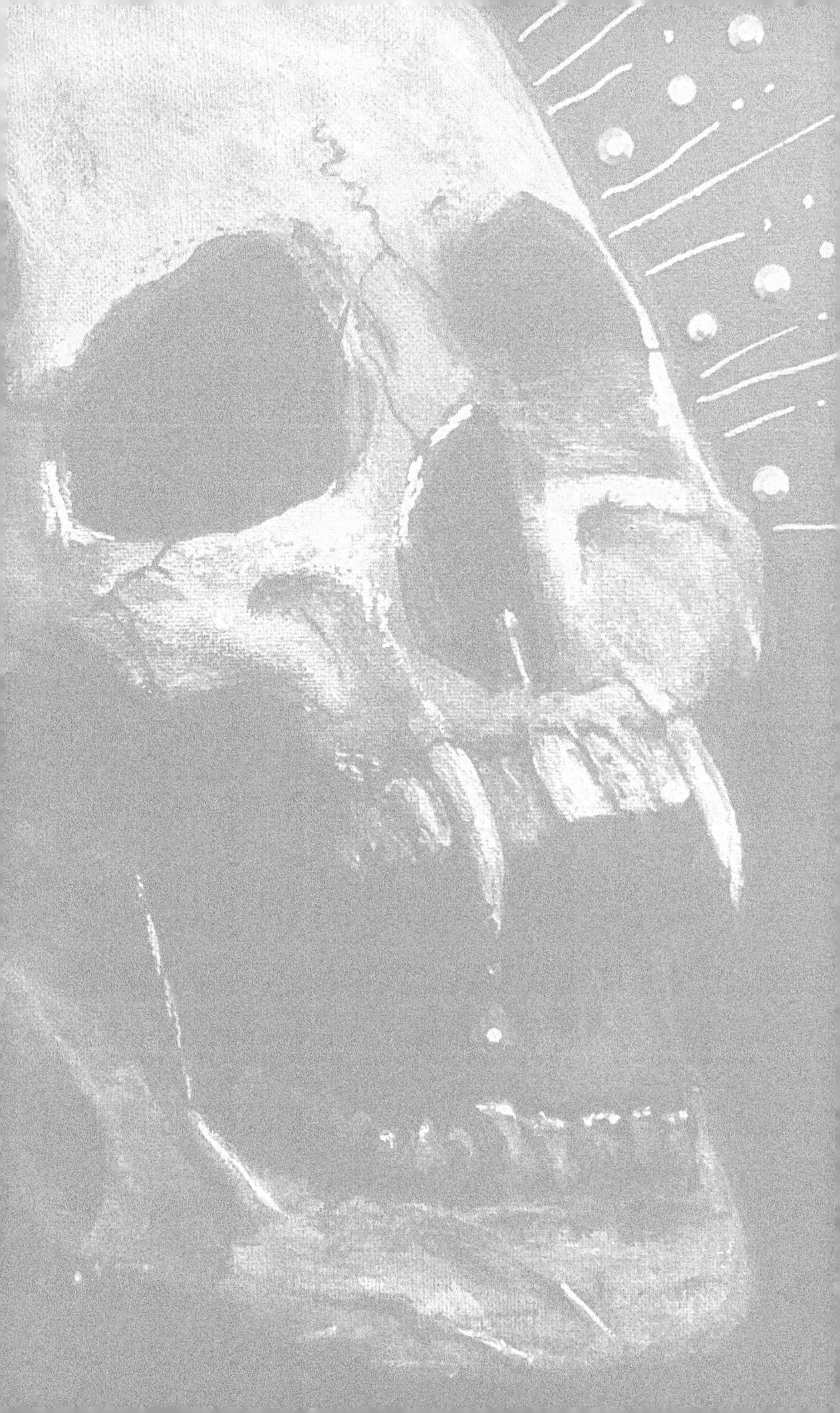

31. Love Lost

I remember your laugh—
The smile you shared.
Your innocence,
It was beautiful, serene,
Like nothing ever seen.

You showed me how to be—
To flourish,
To thrive.
And I took your hand,
Gave you a guide.

Yet, in your anger,
You lashed, ripped and slashed—
Sliced open my heart and left it in parts.
My gasping shriek piercing my own ears,
Clattering into the crimson spilt.

I clawed to escape,

JACK TOWNSON

And you dragged me back in.

I had hoped for so much—
To know you were better,
More.

Yet
I'm just
Another
Face.

Featureless

A place to put another's,
And in your fury,
You forgot who I was to you.

The tears we shed,
The battles won and lost,
The good moments,
The bad.

And you ripped my lips to toss them from the
    floor—
Not willing to hear words anymore.

Just to stand over me,
Beating me
Within
An inch
Of
My life.

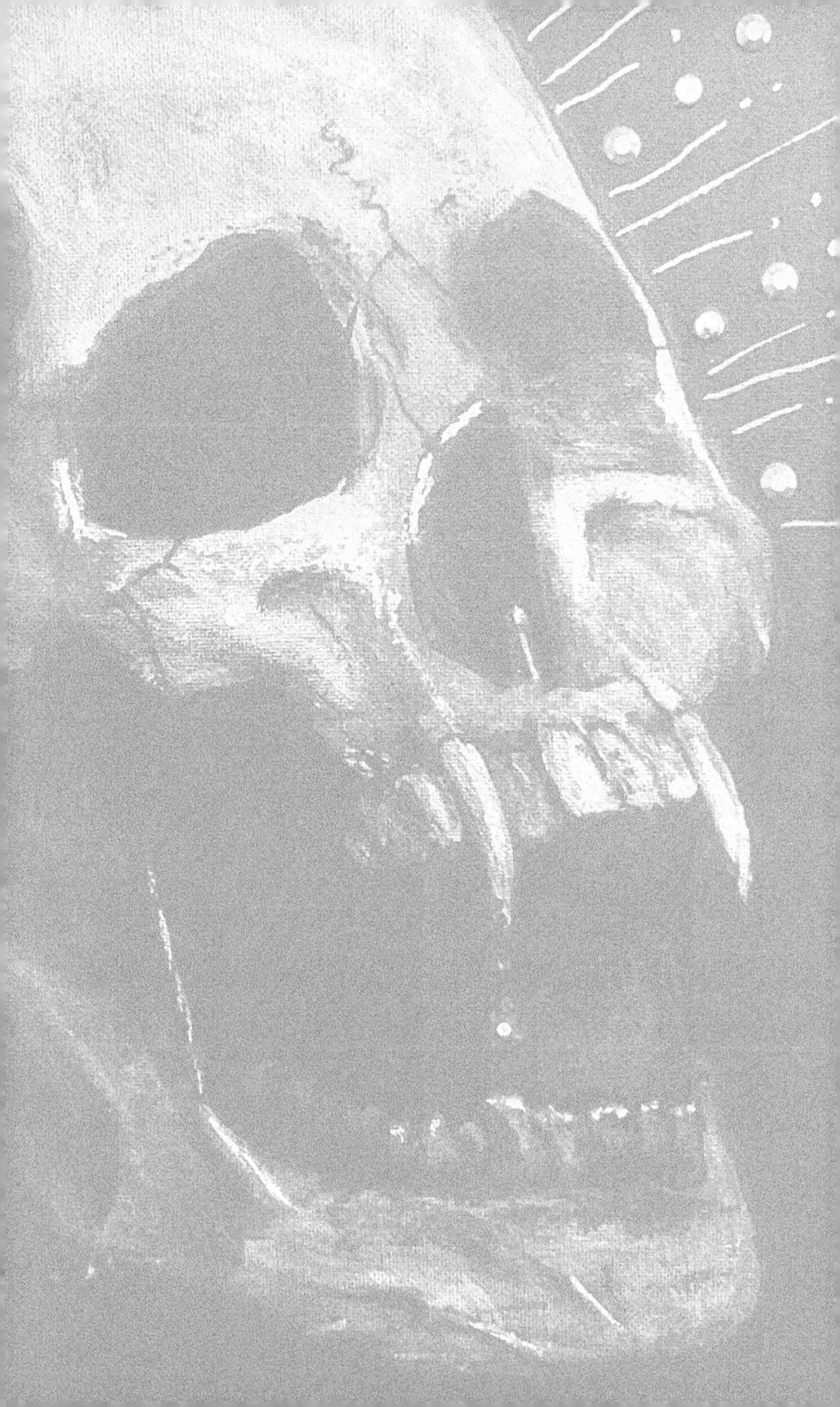

32. Humanity

The world is cruel,
And I was kind.
I gave everything I was to it,
Dear god, I tried.

I fought my battles,
Lost my wars,
Defeat, complete,
Down to the floor.

And I screamed,
As I clutched myself tight,
Wishing to drift back ,
Far into the night.

Where I could be free again,
Yet I was chained to this word:

"Human."

Yet, what does this mean,
To be such a frail creature,
This frail broken thing?

Is it to be petty, ruthless, and cruel,
To stomp on all who don't obey?
Or is it to be loved, in ways so true,
And yes, it does exist—
Flawed, even too.

No.

To be human is none.
Lost and alone,
Yet, loved by the sun.

In all of my years,
And cycles learned,
One truth exposed,
And not one I yearned—

To be human, dear friend,
Is to fight to the end,
While the voices of peers,
Family and friends...

Scream for your downfall,
And wish for your end,
Wishing you nothing to gain,
To fill their own heads,

Silence your words,
And make no amends,

*And so,
I reject you,
Your humanity is nothing.*

A lie.

*And so I wave it away—
Wish it goodbye:
The end of the cycle,
To return to the night,
An end of the suffering.*

*My lifelong plight—
No neglectful father or mother,
No murderous seed,
No womb to cry into,
Tossed out in the street.*

*What I was wasn't wrong—
I fought tooth and nail,
My sword on the floor,
Exhausted and failed.*

*I tried to be good,
Be better than them,
To push nature aside,
To never give in.*

*Yet I couldn't succeed,
And in this, I dread,
Where my road will lead,
It is in ways the end.*

Of the boy I once was,
The kind-hearted friend,
So I'll shun it away,
Locked tight in a box.
This thing called humanity,
With an iron-bound lock.

No more struggling,
No more pain,
No more,
No!

I tried!
God, I tried.
And yet, at each turn,
I'm filled with this fright,
Of the last phoenix burn,
Filling the night with the embers,
Of me.

From the mind of Jack Townson Bestselling Author of *Blood and Roses* comes a poetry anthology dripping with Darkness. Every page filled with nightmares, regrets, agony and torment, sprinkles of dark romance and the descent into becoming a monster. The jaded sibling to the romance filled first volumes of his works, *Death and Lilies* is the beast beneath your bed waiting to drag you to the infernal pits while sharing the deepest and most pained emotions of the writer himself.

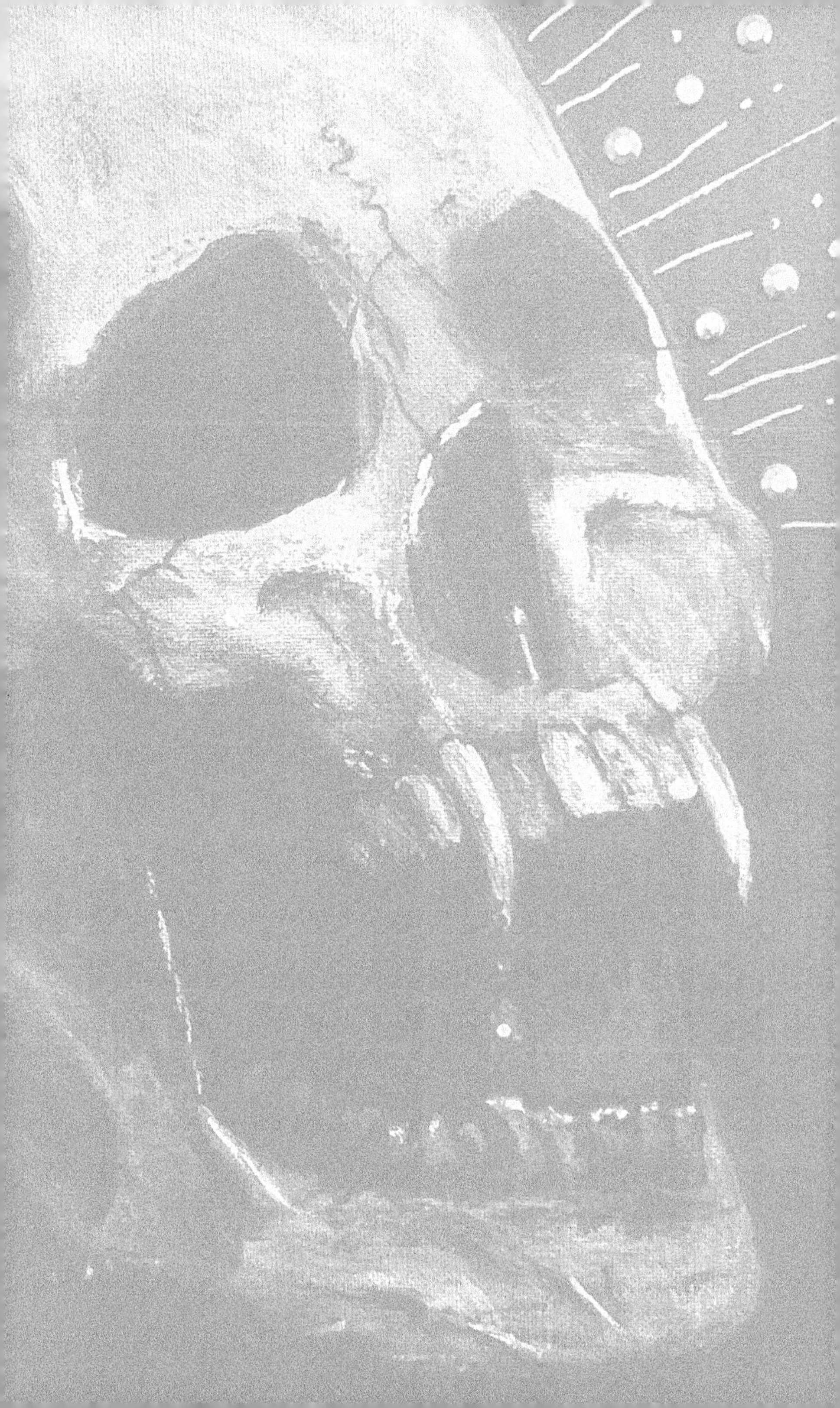

33. The Tapping

Late at night while you're fast asleep,
Eyes shut tight, your breathing steep,
There comes a sound unlike another,
Causing you to rise and shudder.

What, oh what, could this sound be?
A rhythmic tapping resounds hurriedly.
It drums across the walls and doors,
Forcing you to rise with force.

What, oh what, could cause this noise,
And who, pray-tell, would make this choice?
To come into your room at night,
And filling your soul with chilling fright.

Perhaps the cat left beyond the frame,
It's tiny claws scratching your name,
Wishing to be let within,

Jack Townson

To the comfort of sheets and sleep-warmed
	skin.

And with your inspection a realization
	dawns,
That feline friend, it bends and yawns.
Upon your floor you left it last,
The blackened form and fur-filled mass.

It stares upon the entrance's face,
Hair on end, it hears the bass,
Of the tapping sound that started slow,
Now a banging that seems to grow.

The craft wood it groans and shakes,
From the phantom limb smashing its face.
The air once previously calm and soft,
Replaced by a putridity that begins to waft,

Filled the nostrils of your nose,
Of rotten flesh and severed toes.
And oh, the bumps upon your skin,
These tiny pricks of needles' pins,

Signaling the terror-filled,
This knocking now in for the kill,
Your mind, it swims with every thought,
Of the abject terror that has been wrought.

And with a final thrusted push,
The door, it opens, where passed it stood,
A monster of abnormal size,
Its body shriveled, and crimson eyes.

Hunched its back, its spine protrudes,
Bony talons to slice right through;
A dripping drool catches the light,
Warm, fresh liquid drips out of sight.

The feline friend from long before,
Gone in a flash, loyalty ignored.
And there, it waltzes into view,
A demonic malformation comes right
   for you.

An outstretched claw to pull you clear,
Your feet, they kick within your fear,
And the terror comes in waves of shock,
As you hear the room's door lock.

There, behind they cheer and toast,
Your parents' smile, and joyful boast,
"So glad we summoned this hideous beast,
Now let's sit back, enjoy the feast."

34. The Diamond

*She twirls in light,
Like diamonds strung on silk strings.*

*This shining thing— almost too perfect to attain,
And I, a beast, am too dull to compare.*

*She is beauty incarnate,
Like the sun I can never touch.
And in the same way as those damnable rays,
Her soft caress will never bless my horrid skin.*

*She is perfection—
Like a breeze on a summer day,
Giving that moment of relief when the heat becomes too much.*

And just as always, we are not the same,
I am the storm that swallows the sun,
And brings the cold that ruins beach-filled
    enjoyment.

I could never intrude on her life.
For in mine, I am broken...
Alone...
Discarded...
In constant battle with my own demons,
And those sent to destroy me.

I will instead sit in the darkness,
And watch from afar,
Dreaming of a day
I could call
Her
Mine.

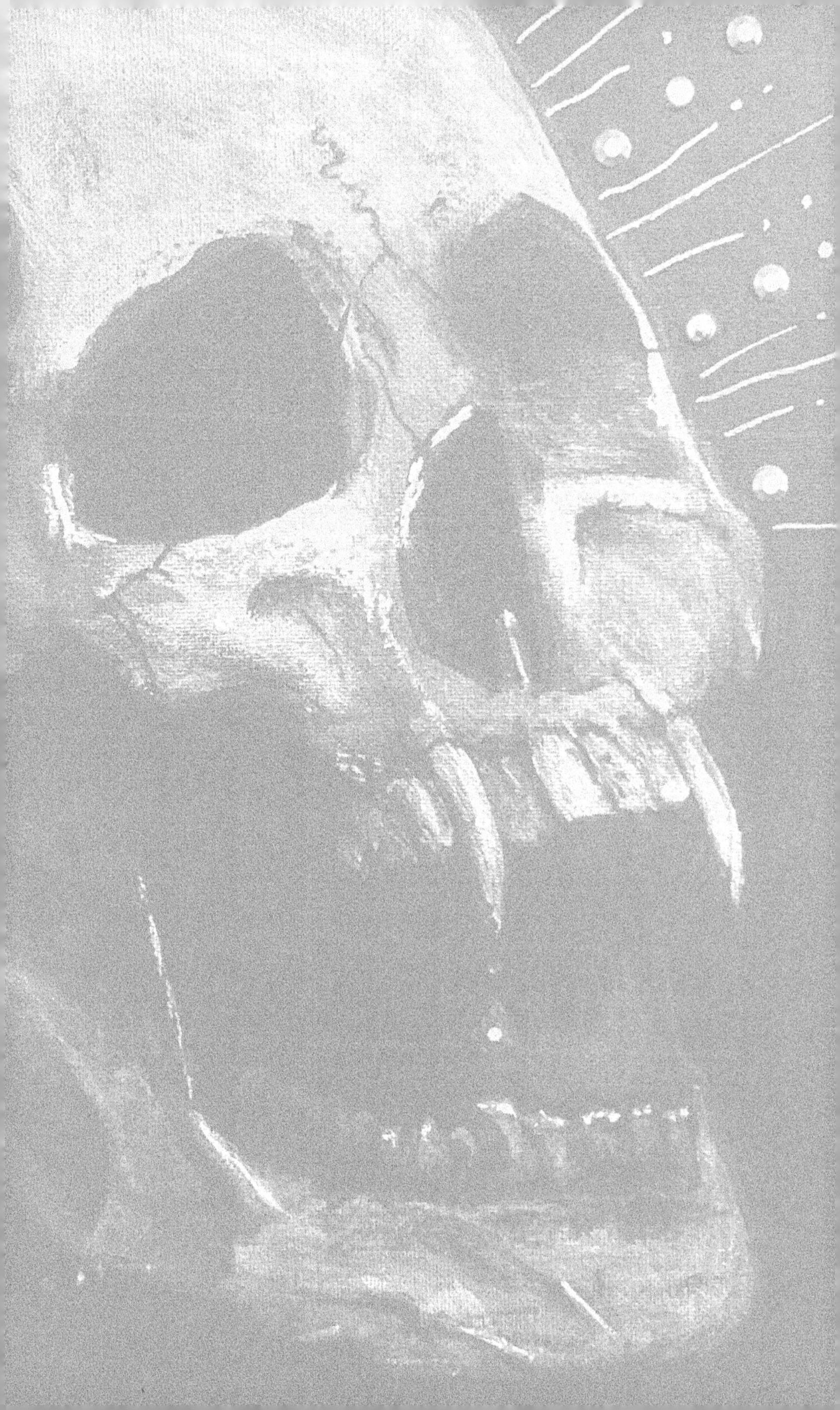

35. The Clock

Ticktock, ticktock—
The noise it goes,
The old hands twitch,
Its chime echoes.

Signaling the sound of doom,
The funeral marches towards your tomb,
And as it fills your ears with song,
Your family, they all sing along.

"Ticktock, ticktock,
We knew her well.
A shame she now resides in hell,
Where demons pick upon her corpse,
Where her cries find no remorse.

"She should have known to live her life,
To cause no others pain and strife,
Alas, sweet dear, she hardly knew,

That the reaper knows, he watches too.

"Like Santa towards his Christmas Day,
That all of us, each one must pay,
For the crimes we commit and subject
    others too,
She didn't think, her mind too shrewd."

"A shame," one speaks, with dulcet tones.
"A shame the clock had to be tolled!"

The clock, the clock, it rings with glee,
Ticktock sounds chiming violently.
All though, alas, none else would hear,
Besides the corpse of said sweet dear.

And she hears it, don't worry, she truly does,
A sound of horror that never rusts,
Shining bright through her torment,
To remind her of the transgressions she
    refused to relent.

"Oh what, dear God, did I do to deserve?"
You beg, you plead, your mind, it swerves.

"Simple," a response comes clear as day.
"You were hardly good, you had to pay.
For, on our death beds we find the truth,
Of the crimes we commit long gone since
    youth.

"And weighed they are for all to see,
Your family, your friends, and even... me!

And in this judgment, you must realize,
That there is no bias, no single lie.

"Your words and actions are held close
 to you,
For they are your jury, no peers... just you."

36. Silhouette

Hairs raise against your neck,
Urging fear to rise at the beck.
And with the turn in said direction,
Twin orbs glow in the reflection,

Of the light that barely passes,
Through the eerie smoke-filled masses,
Undulating just out of frame,
Of your eyes as they fail their aim.

It matters not just what you're doing.
You feel the darkness gently brewing,
Just out of focus of your vision,
Questioning your sights precision.

Your mind, it wanders to every thought,
Of the thing that lurks just out of thought.
Oh horror, oh humanity, what could it be?
This thing that has clearly come for thee...

A creature that awaits in dark,
Waiting for a moment's spark.
And with the terror of the moment,
You imagine your final opponent,

As it prepares its true intent,
And inflict grievous harm in an attempt,
To leap upon your broken bones,
And rip away the life you owned.

Clearly, a fiend sent to claim,
Drag away what it has maimed,
And sucking down your putrid soul,
As your cries drift crudely from your home.

Or, perhaps, you'll never know,
Its eyes, a black stare that's filled with woe,
Hoping for the chance to see,
When its dear friend will surely leave.

So it may claim the place it lived,
When life did fill its narrow skin,
And remember what it once was like...
To be just
Like
You.

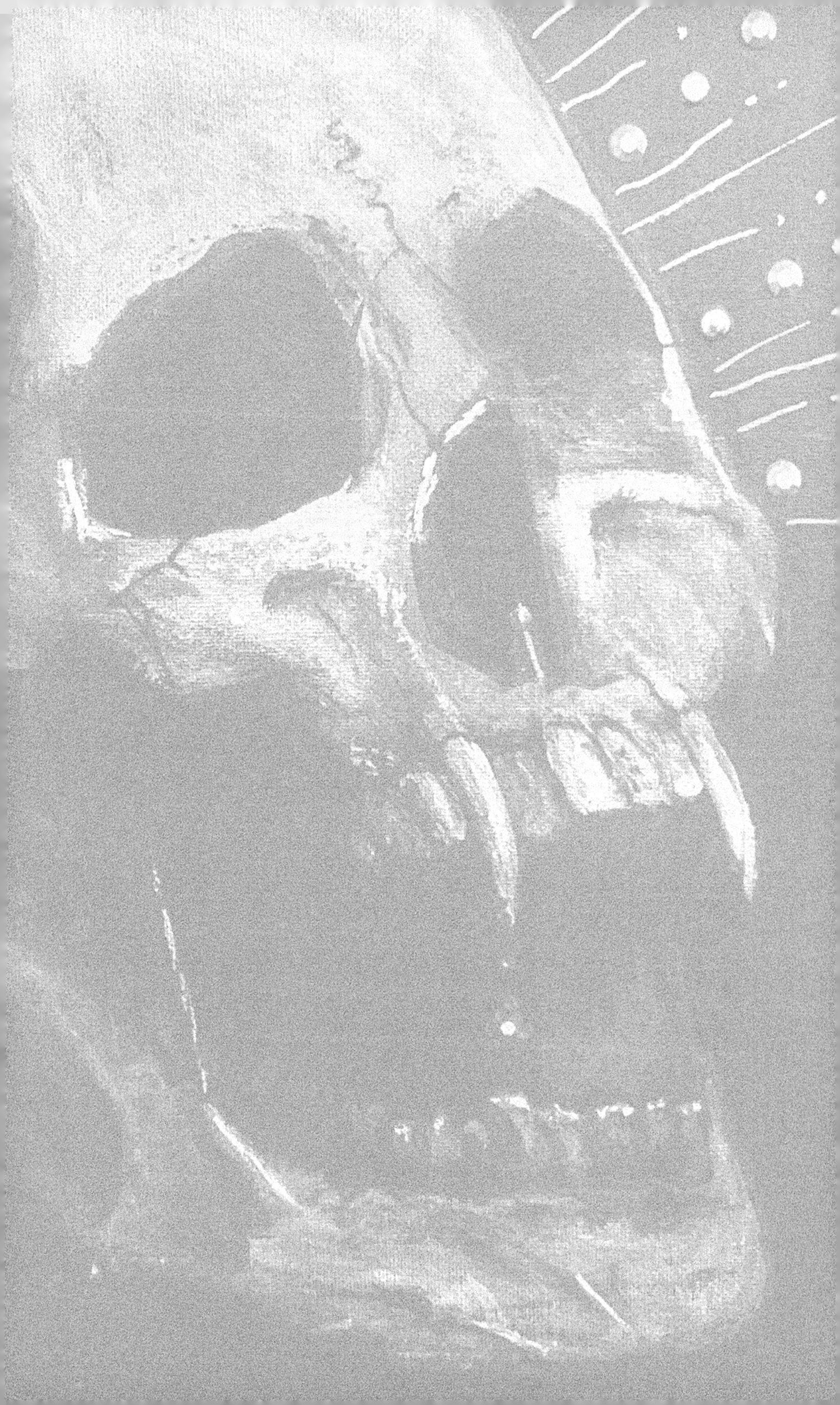

37. Sympathy for the Devil

A dark knight watches from the edge of reality,
Bushy brows furrowed with a crimson gaze,
Armor covered in rust, where once, a brilliant silver shined.

A single blackened wing outstretched, it is broken—his feathers a mess.
Once, he was God's favorite—now, a ronin,
An outcast.

A wandering warrior scanning the depths of the underworld,
He knew his purpose, his place— a mighty sword to send foes scattering;
A duty he gladly took upon in his father's name,
And yet, he was cast aside from favorite to former—

*No longer seen as a hero, but as a serpent
 sent to corrupt.*
*Yet is he truly the sinner, or is he more the
 saint?*
The answer is neither.

*He is the roaring flame that brings light to
 the world,*
*Illuminates minds and sets them free from
 the chains of rigidness,*
To show us truly what is possible.

Is he anger, or patience?
Is he fear, or bravery?
Is he false idol, or icon?
Is he hatred, or love?

A devil
With horns
To raise
Us
Up.

About the Author

The Vampire Jack Townson is an actor, live-action role-player, and vampfluencer based on Long Island, New York with a dedicated following on social media of over thirty thousand people. Jack Townson is also a celebrated recording artist and author, but his most important role in his unlife is the one he takes most seriously...father.

For more information about the works of Jack Townson
and upcoming novel series, visit:
www.vampirejacktownson.com

THE VAMPIRE
Jack
Townson

Milton Keynes UK
Ingram Content Group UK Ltd.
UKHW020617241023
431227UK00011B/315